Wendy,
It's been a

hang out virtually with you.
Looking forward to doing it,
one day in person.

I hope you enjoy my
ramblings.

Deserve's Got Nothing
To Do With It

Much Love,

Charlie

ENDORSEMENTS

"Charlie Midnight's book, *Deserve's Got Nothing To Do With It,* has the ring of truth on every page. It is a no-BS, no-sugarcoating, no-grandstanding guide to survival in the music business. It's an irreverent, fun read that gives budding musicians and songwriters a heads-up while offering artists with decades of mastery the chance to recognize themselves, reflect on their careers, and come away heartened and inspired. Charlie has been in the top tier of songwriters and producers for decades. This is the straight dope about what it takes to remain creative for a lifetime—not just the first album."

Mark Bryan, Co-founder of *The Artist's Way* workshops

"Charlie Midnight gives us a practical guide, demonstrating that genuine success is measured as much as what we contribute to the world around us as by what we gain in money and titles. The world needs more CRAPP from Charlie Midnight!"

Peter Hirsch, Social entrepreneur, attorney-at-law, network marketing pro, and bestselling author of *Living with Passion: 10 Simple Secrets that Guarantee Your Success*

"Charlie Midnight's *Deserve's Got Nothing To Do With It* is absolutely inspiring, empowering, and serious fun. In our global education initiatives, it helps us to understand the power of believing in your self-worth and the value of pursuing and persevering in your own aspirations. His book reaches into the soul of what you experience in the music industry, giving you riveting stories about his circuitous path to success that will light up the darkest times in your own journey. The five elements of CRAPP are a guide on how to survive, keep fighting, and manage the quagmire of endless possible curves and directions that may discourage you when chasing your dream in any field. This book is an enjoyable and rewarding educational experience."

Karen D. Reed, CEO and president of KDR Global Education Solutions

"Deserve's Got Nothing To Do With It should be mandatory reading for every aspiring songwriter, as well as anyone interested in learning about the nexus where tenacity and perseverance conjoin with divine inspiration. For decades, Charlie Midnight has remained in the upper echelon of songwriting royalty. His fertile imagination, combined with his relentless quest to conjure the perfect word or phrase to convey a thought with clarity, insight, rhyme, and reason, is endlessly exhilarating. Charlie makes an ideal collaborator because he intuitively understands the power of exchanging ideas to make a song deeply personal, while at the same time, universally relatable. Key to his success is his ability to embrace every musical genre, from the greatest traditional singers and contemporary teen pop stars, to the giants of R&B and rock and roll."

Jay Landers, Legendary A&R Managing Executive Producer and A&R for Barbra Streisand for 27 albums to date. Executive Producer and A&R for albums that have sold in excess of 100 million copies in the US alone. These recordings have garnered multiple Grammy awards (including 30 nominations in the Grammy's "Best Traditional Pop Album" category), Emmy awards, Golden Globes, and Oscar "Best Song" winners.

"Reading *Deserve's Got Nothing To Do With It* was like reading an emotional MRI of my life. My father used to always tell me there is no substitute for experience. Life doesn't work off a set of hard rules, but experience is a good predictor of future behavior. Charlie's sensitivities to human behavior and life lessons gives us a chance to learn through him. I've traveled through a broad array of experiences in my lifetime: from my street days in the tough neighborhood of Brooklyn, to the cockpit of a commercial airliner where I sat as an airline captain for over two decades, to being selected as a flight candidate for the NASA space program, attending law school, becoming an inventor with over 40 patents, surviving the infomercial business, becoming a real estate owner and operator, and then founding my own record label where I first met Charlie, I know what it takes to navigate the ups and downs of life.

Charlie has been able to use his emotional net to capture and organize how a relationship can affect all our dealings. He creates a coherent road map, and when used correctly, can be applied to anyone's travels through life. As someone who has been down many different roads, I see his lessons in all my dealings. I only wish he had written this book decades ago, so that I could have benefited from the many lessons. I urge anyone that dreams of reaching beyond the limits of their office or bedroom window to read this book."

Harry Zimmerman, CEO of 11 Harbor Records

TESTIMONIALS FROM LECTURES

"The group was BLOWN AWAY. No kidding—one of the best presentations we have had in a long time!"

Jeffrey Rabhan, Chair, Tisch School of the Arts,
Clive Davis Institute of Recorded Music

"Charlie's lecture was one of the most inspiring speeches I have heard in quite some time, and the emails and feedback he received from my students was absolute proof."

Bruce Perlmutter, Senior Vice President at Condé Nast Entertainment

"Informative, funny, and absolutely motivational."

Nikki Mirasola, Events Coordinator, Tisch School of the
Arts, Clive Davis Institute of Recorded Music

"The ambition and drive and willingness to never stop until you get what you want is something I call a 'person's pilot light.' When that pilot light gets ignited, there is no stopping the furnace from burning. Charlie has poured gasoline all over my pilot light...I appreciate the fire he's stoked in my belly. I know anything can be accomplished with a lot of CRAPP."

JP Amato, Student, Syracuse University

"I know I speak for everyone when I say that your discussion really hit home for a group of people trying to break into the entertainment industry."

Tara McHugh, Student, Syracuse University

MASCOT® BOOKS

www.mascotbooks.com

Deserve's Got Nothing To Do With It: Five Elements That Will Help You Survive Your Emotional Journey to Success

For more information, please contact:
Mascot Books
620 Herndon Parkway #320
Herndon, VA 20170
info@mascotbooks.com

Library of Congress Control Number: 2020916710

CPSIA Code: PRV0321A
ISBN-13: 978-1-68401-835-2

Printed in the United States

DESERVE'S

Got **Nothing** To Do With It

Five Elements That Will Help You Survive
Your Emotional Journey to Success

Talking CRAPP With
CHARLIE MIDNIGHT

For my wife, Susanna, my daughters Hannah and Shantie, my mother and father, Bella and Leo Kaufman, may they rest in peace, and the late genius Dan Hartman, who handed me a career.

PROLOGUE

In the classic Western *Unforgiven*, there is a scene with a line of dialogue that informs and simplifies much of my existential philosophy on how to accept the indifference of the universe to get what you think you deserve.

In the scene, Will Munny (Clint Eastwood) has come to avenge the murder of his great friend, Ned Logan (Morgan Freeman), who had been unjustly whipped to death by Sheriff Little Bill Daggett (Gene Hackman). Little Bill is lying wounded on the floor of the saloon, and Will Munny has a shotgun pointed at Bill's head. Anticipating the impending blast, Bill's face clenches and flattens in fear as if he is being suppressed by a mighty g-force. Little Bill says, "I don't deserve this...to die like this. I was building a house." Will replies, "Deserve's got nothing to do with it," and pulls the trigger, leaving Little Bill's house to stand unfinished.

That is the gist of the attitude that has stopped me from measuring my success, or lack thereof, against someone else's. If deserve's got nothing to do with it, then what does? Talent? Opportunity? Persistence? Luck? All of it? None of it? Make up your own list, and it will fit into someone's experience.

INTRODUCTION

*There is no passion to be found playing
small—in settling for a life that is less
than the one you are capable of living.*

NELSON MANDELA

This is not a motivational book. I am not writing this to motivate you, but rather to address those of you who are already
motivated. Furthermore, let's accept that everyone has talent
and would love to have success in their chosen fields.

The idea for this book evolved from the many times I
have sat with people who work in a variety of occupations and
inspired them to follow their dreams. Holding up my career
as an example, I demonstrated it was possible, even probable,
that they would carve out the career they dreamed of if they
had the determination. Those I mentored and inspired told me

many times that I should write a book and spread the word, so I thought about how I could succinctly describe what I was constantly speaking about and created the acronym CRAPP:

Collaboration
Relationships
Ambition
Passion
Persistence

I decided to also include my thoughts about songwriting in this book, but more as a meditation on following your muse and developing your strengths than a guide about how to write a song.

Music has provided me with my career, but I believe my philosophies and thoughts can help anyone in any career. Our career paths may be different, but the elements in my book are universal and can help anyone get through personal struggles and ultimately achieve success.

I draw my opinions from thirty years of working as a songwriter and record producer with more than a few notable achievements. From this, I present the elements and strategies that I believe will help you transcend the pitfalls, setbacks, naysayers, and self-doubts that can stymie you.

It has been my good fortune to have written and produced songs for such artists as Barbra Streisand, Andrea Bocelli, to Joni Mitchell, James Brown, Joe Cocker, Chaka Khan, Idina Menzel, Cher, Christina Aguilera, Britney Spears, Hilary Duff, Anastacia, the Doobie Brothers, Billy Joel, Jamey Johnson, and many others. My songs have been heard in over forty films, including

The Bodyguard, Rocky IV, Bull Durham, Burlesque, Harry and the Hendersons, Great Expectations, and *Cloudy with a Chance of Meatballs.* I wrote the theme song for the Nickelodeon show *Big Time Rush* and have had my songs covered and uploaded on YouTube by people who do not necessarily know my name but know my work. I had a spectacularly unsuccessful career as a recording artist, but by using the principles of CRAPP, I was able to survive and then thrive as a record producer and songwriter.

The elements of CRAPP do not guarantee success but will, I believe, help you to maximize your chances for success; and by *success* I mean having a career doing what you love to do—waking up in the morning and looking forward to your day's work.

> *If you choose a job you love, you will never work a day in your life.*
>
> **CONFUCIUS**

It is my hope that CRAPP will resonate with those of you looking for guidance on a journey to success that can feel overwhelming and defeating, like driving to the Promised Land with no road map or GPS and arriving at a crossroads where the sign says "Your Guess Is as Good as Mine."

In my younger days, I had many jobs that I needed but did not love: working in the dairy aisle of Waldbaum's; unloading trains in upstate New York in the middle of winter; being a legal proofreader and a paralegal; acting as a bouncer in a pool hall; serving as an attendant in a massage parlor; mailing out diet books called *From Soup to Nuts*; and working in a men's clothing store as the worst salesman ever. After all these odd jobs, I have been able to make my living by writing and producing music, and by Confucius's definition, I haven't worked a day.

There are things I remember which may never have happened but as I recall them so they take place.

HAROLD PINTER

Since I have never kept a journal to record moments or thoughts as they've occurred, I will not swear to the accuracy of the anecdotes contained herein, since even writing in a diary does not ensure the veracity of memory. As a result, I am comfortable going forward and relating my stories with that quote from *Old Times* by Harold Pinter leading the way.

When I was nine years old, I had a confrontation with a boy named Jimmy in the schoolyard of PS 186 on Seventy-Sixth Street in Bensonhurst. The schoolyard was a block away from my house, a distance that allowed me to walk to and from school each day by myself. Jimmy was twelve years old and significantly bigger than me both in height and girth. We were playing a half-court game of basketball, and when I was dribbling the ball, Jimmy pushed me to the ground, took the ball, and scored a basket. Instinctively, I jumped up, rushed toward Jimmy, and punched him in the face. Then I ran, faster than a speeding bullet, down Seventy-Sixth Street and across Nineteenth Avenue, avoiding by inches a 1959 red-and-white Chevrolet Kingswood station wagon. Not looking back, I reached my house, where my mother, Bella, was standing at the top of the stoop, wearing a flower-print apron and smoking a Kool cigarette that dangled from her bottom lip.

I bent over for a moment, sweating, with my hands on my knees, trying to catch my breath and listening for the sound of Jimmy's footsteps. Quickly, I straightened up and walked up the stoop toward my mother. As I was about to reach for the door handle to escape into the safety of my house, Bella pushed my hand aside, thwarting my entrance, and asked, "Why are you running?"

"Let me in, Mom, and I'll tell you."

"Tell me, and maybe I'll let you in."

"Mom, let me in, please," I pleaded.

"Stop whining, and tell me the truth."

I tried once more to get past my mother, but she prevailed. "Why are you running?"

I looked behind me, down the block, and there was no sign of Jimmy. But I knew that he would be coming for me. "I got into a fight with Jimmy," I said, still trying to ease my way through the door. An ash from her cigarette fell from her lip onto my head. She disdained my futile attempt to bypass her.

"Did you start the fight?" she asked.

My mother had once caught me in a lie when I had tried changing a failing grade on my report card to a passing one by rubbing the original with a pencil eraser. I had rubbed so hard that there was a slight hole in the card, but I still managed to scrawl in a respectable B.

"Did you change your grade?" she had asked. It was clear to me that I had not fooled her, yet I replied, "No."

It was better to tell the truth to Bella than to lie to her. My reward for lying had been a bar of soap in my mouth and a warning that young liars become adult liars, and adult liars become criminals, and criminals end up in jail. Then my mother had sealed the deal by saying, "You keep lying, and you'll take ten years off my life. Your children should only do to you what you do to me."

When I first started driving, I took our Chevy Impala to pick up my girlfriend at school, and while double parked, waiting for her to emerge, I forgot to put the car in park. I took my foot off the brake and reached across the seat to open the passenger-side door; in doing so, my hand turned the steering wheel toward the curb and the car slammed into a parked Buick Special, caving in its driver-side door.

There were many witnesses to my major embarrassment, and I left a note on the windshield with my telephone number, which, of course, I would have done regardless. When I got home, I told my mother what happened, apologizing, chastising myself, and promising to forego, forever, driving the car.

"Are you hurt?" she asked.

"No," I answered.

"Thank God you're okay. You can drive the car. It's good to get back on the horse after you've fallen off." Bella then kissed me on the head in the same spot that the ash had once fallen. "Charlesey," she said, "material things can be replaced."

I did not lie to my mother on the day of the Jimmy fight as she stood on the top step of the stoop, blocking my way.

"Tell the truth," she insisted, reminding me of the bar of soap awaiting the mouth of a liar.

Brushing the ash off my head, feeling a profound sense of guilt, and hoping for sanctuary, I said, "I started the fight."

"Keep running," she said.

I stumbled slightly backward in shock. "Because I started the fight?" I asked.

"Yes," she replied.

"Mommy, please, I won't do it again," I said with the most imploring look I could muster.

"Whine all you want—it won't help."

"But I told the truth," I reasoned.

"That's why you won't get a bar of soap in your mouth," she said with perfect logic. So I ran.

This is a story I have told many times over about the way I learned to take responsibility for my actions and how my mother was so tough that one of my friends named her Bella the Barracuda. It is a story that, as I remember it, was the foundation of my belief that I am probably in whatever dire straits I find myself because of myself, at least partially, and blaming someone or something else serves no purpose. If you cannot see how your choices and actions have led you to the unwanted predicament you are in, then you are doomed to repeat those choices and actions and constantly find yourself in the same bad place.

I did not learn that lesson right away and cannot recall exactly when I truly integrated my enlightened perspective into my world view. Perhaps that moment of clarity will burst into my consciousness one day as a newly revealed memory and a welcome addition to the stories of my journey. I already hear Bella's voice at the close of the anecdote reminding me to "stop whining."

It was decades later when I started regaling people with this tale of Bella the Stoop Sentinel, and I am not sure if I remember the details as they were or as I reimagined them. I am clear that I started a fight, that I fled the scene, and that Bella told me to run. I am also sure that my mother flicked ash onto my head at some point in my youth, which she could have done for any number of my missteps. I am almost positive that I did have to dodge a car as I flew across the broad expanse of Nineteenth Avenue, and that car was a red-and-white Chevrolet Kingswood station wagon.

Each of these memories is indelible, cinematic, and true—true to the spirit of the event. I see each moment vividly—the colors, the cars, and the schoolyard. I remember Jimmy's face, splotched with pimples bursting red with anger. I must have glimpsed that face in the split second between the punch and my terror-fueled mad dash out of the schoolyard.

Memory is an untrustworthy biographer. The more time passes, the blurrier or more colorful the scenarios of your life can become. Sometimes they disappear until your reality is that they never occurred. Sometimes they appear eons after they have occurred, and you question if they are simply inventions, but they play so vividly in your mind that you accept that they happened, at least in a similar way.

And how do you check the accuracy of your remembrances? Even a visual recording can be open to interpretation, and interpretation can be a product of imagination and inclination. Nevertheless, I stand by my memories as accurate portrayals of the meanings and visual essences of the incidents, because when I try to understand why I have certain feelings, beliefs, and attitudes, those memories emerge as bridges that connect what I have experienced and what I have, for better or worse, become.

There are no facts, only interpretations.
FRIEDRICH NIETZSCHE

The way I wrote this book is the way of my journey: zigzag, and keep pushing onward. Although I cannot vouch for the complete accuracy of every detail in the book, the essence is true; at least it is true for me. Sometimes it will be a stream of consciousness that ends up at a place that surprises me.

I wrote anecdotes, as they came to me, that supported the points I was making. There was little calculation in choosing what and whom to write about. I include specific companions and collaborators in the retelling based on how well the anecdotes support what I want to say and not because other friends and collaborators are less important to me.

Chapter One
BENSONHURST

I'm from Bensonhurst, a working-class neighborhood where the richest guy on the block owned his own cab. The second richest was a waiter at a fancy restaurant in the borough of Manhattan—the borough that we in Brooklyn called "the city." I went to a high school called Lafayette, which no longer exists. They closed it down because it became too violent.

I quit Brooklyn College after three semesters and left for England with a rock-and-roll band. My mother said I took ten years off her life, but she lived to the age of ninety-three. I never accomplished anything with the band but frequented many clubs in London trying to be part of the scene. I also spent some time trying to pick up girls on Carnaby Street. In both of those endeavors, I was blithely persistent but unsuccessful. I came home months later and began my arduous journey toward success, knowing nothing except that I wanted to be the lead singer in a rock-and-roll band—not a completely original idea, but complete originality is overrated and a long-gone possibility.

My experience has been that my creations owe something to the songs and writings that I have heard and read. Sometimes I recognize my influences, but that is not always the case. Still, I know that my idea is not wholly original and did not come from a big bang out of nothingness. It is the product of my imagination processing whatever elements I have digested and filtered through my idiosyncrasies, emotions, objectives, passions, and desires to create something great in my own "original voice."

Having your own original voice that is recognizable among countless other "original voices" is an attainable and inspired goal.

Having a completely original idea that is not dependent upon any ideas that came before might be possible, but it is not as important as wanting to create something great in your unique voice.

INNOCENT BYSTANDER

In 1982, the Charlie Midnight *Innocent Bystander* album was released on the Columbia/Decent Records label. There was a record-release party at Billy and Elizabeth Joel's massive apartment on Central Park South in New York City. I recall that the entire record company was there to celebrate, but my memories of those days may be colored by a bit of wishful thinking. Still, I am sure that Billy played piano and sang and I had felt certain that after all the dues I had paid—after all the bars, clubs, and rehearsals; the six sets a night; and the forty-on-twenty-off gigs playing "Mustang Sally" at 2:00 a.m. to a crowd of five in Brooklyn emporiums like the Half Inn—my well-deserved rock-and-roll stardom was imminent.

It was not.

The album bombed, and the band was dropped from the label.

My album, *Innocent Bystander*, was a colossal commercial failure. It sold almost no albums and got almost no airplay except, if I remember correctly, in Brownsville, Texas, where the radio station was kind enough or, possibly, the only one in the United States with good music taste ... or desperate enough to take whatever perks were offered to play my songs (a practice rumored to exist in those halcyon days of the music business). Getting added to the radio playlist in Brownsville was a high point of the album release, which was followed almost immediately with one of the many low points. In this particular instance, the Brownsville station had a "win a date with Charlie Midnight" contest. I, of course, showed up to have a date with one of my ardent admirers, who I am sure had a lucid moment and never appeared.

I went on tour with my band, starting with a big send off in New York City and ending with a big apathetic shrug in Los Angeles, California. The drive back east was a moribund trek toward reality: we were not going to be on the cover of *Rolling Stone* magazine unless they planned an issue featuring "The Ten Worst Tours Behind a Major Label Album Release in the History of Rock." This was not a great time for me. *Unforgiven* had not yet been filmed, but I was definitely in the state of mind that I deserved better. It is from these moments that philosophies evolve.

At the time, I was unaware of being in an evolutionary phase. In a few months, I had gone from becoming the rock star of my dreams to the pariah of the record company, the radio stations, and the music venues. It hurt and seemed inexplicable that, after all those years of striving, the end could come so quickly. The total failure of the album felt like a poison that was spreading through my system, breaking down the sinew of confidence that had lifted me up and kept me going for so many years.

When you feel the anguish of unexpected and crushing rejection, it is difficult to not feel sorry for yourself. "Why me? I don't deserve this" is a normal response. When you look around at others and compare what appears to be their success to your own perceived failure, you might say, "Why them and not me?" But in reply to that entreaty to the universe, Bella would simply say, "Stop whining."

Bella's invocation notwithstanding, I walked listlessly through the streets of Manhattan feeling lost, shifting between feeling nothing, feeling resigned, and feeling angry. I slogged from my East Village stomping grounds, past the junkie holdovers from the Woodstock Nation strumming their guitars in Washington Square, and stopped at a vendor on Eighth Avenue and Thirty-Seventh Street to buy a new pair of two-dollar shades—sometimes the world looks better when viewed through dark glasses. Feeling slightly better, I turned east down Forty-Second Street, where the X-rated movie theaters pimped their films and the available ladies generously offered dates. Then I headed uptown on Broadway, checking out the teeming varieties of life forms from behind my cool new sunglasses.

There were many people I did not know and who did not know of my failed album; some looked at me and smiled. "It must be the shades," I thought and felt a little spring in my step as I did the Bensonhurst Bop all the way to Central Park, the most beautiful oasis on earth.

Strolling through the streets of Manhattan has always been a cure for my dark moods. It is, for me, healing to realize that I am only one of billions of people who may be aspiring toward something. I had not yet solidified my credo, "deserve's got nothing to do with it," but as I recall the sequence of emotions I felt as I made my way to Central Park, I recognize the seeds of the philosophy that has helped me soldier on.

I sat down on the east side of the lake and removed my shades to fully savor the view of the timeless trees surrounded by buildings that rose surrealistically behind them—a singular landscape that never failed to lighten my heart. I saw a pretty girl walking my way, and I put my shades back in place. There is no justification for whining when you are alive and in the presence of so much beauty. The girl smiled at me and kept walking out of the park and into my memories.

I came home from the endless trudge of the tour, and the record label did not offer us a second album. It was over. Now what? I started working the graveyard shift for law firms as a temp proofreader of legal documents. It was a good job that paid the rent, and it bought a ticket to a movie and a bowl of barley soup and some challah bread at the Vesulka restaurant in New York's East Village. I was feeling good and had put some musicians together for a new band. Then I got the call that I felt I deserved, not yet realizing that deserve's got nothing to do with it.

Chapter Two

CRAPP

Question: When is crap not crap?

Answer: When it is CRAPP—collaboration, relationships, ambition, passion, and persistence.

TURNING CRAP INTO CRAPP

I did not start pursuing my career with these ideas and philosophies. CRAPP emerged out of a determination to survive the constant roadblocks, disappointments, and defeats. Perhaps if the arc of my journey had been different, I would have developed a different outlook. Perhaps if my album had been successful, I would have written a different book about how, by projecting my rock stardom, I had become a rock star and called it, *My Destiny,* but I arrived where I am now not by destiny.

It was through grit, blind faith, and finding the satisfactions along the way that gave me joy during the process, regardless of the frustrations and how bleak a particular moment may have seemed. Out of a desire to live in a state of mind where my life would not be validated only if I reached a certain level of success (as defined by others who didn't know me), I had an epiphany: the creating—the doing—has to be an end in itself.

When I was living on the border of Coney Island, Brooklyn, in a ground-floor, one-bedroom apartment, sleeping on a mattress on the floor next to a plastic garbage bag full of my clothes, I had to nail down the windows so that it would be harder for my druggie friends to break in. Some days, I would walk to the abandoned winter beach, climb onto an empty lifeguard chair, and look out at the endless gray ocean of Bay 7 as the icy, wet wind stung my face. I did not feel small and insignificant in the face of such vastness but knew that, like everyone and everything, I could be annihilated in an instant by the power of a nonjudgmental, uncaring universe. Here I had another epiphany: we are all on equal footing, deserving nothing more than the next person and just as much as anyone else. That thought warmed me against the pervasive chill, and I felt peaceful and hopeful. It seems that when the going gets tough, the tough get epiphanies.

I have learned to never look back and say, "What if?" but to look around and say, "What now?" and then to look ahead and say, "What next?" I am satisfied with where I have arrived and believe that my journey is a universal one, common to most people who start out chasing a dream and never expect that pursuit to be as difficult as it turns out to be.

Hopefully a bit of my own story will feel familiar to you and create a bond between us that will reinforce the idea that "If he can do it, so can I." Although my personal experience has been in entertainment, I believe that the elements of my experience I am going to discuss can be applied to any field.

There are doomsayers in the music arena bemoaning the vast changes in the music business and music-technology landscape brought about by digital recording and the ubiquitous internet; they complain it is now harder to earn a living.

But we were not given a birthright to earn a living making music.

Humans have been making music for tens of thousands of years. It is technology that has democratized the concept of having a career in music, and technology is an unstoppable juggernaut.

The question should not be, "How do you think you're going to make a living as a songwriter, or record producer, or recording engineer, or (fill in the blank)?" But, instead, "Why are you pursuing this, and do you have the right attitude and the tools you will need to maximize your chances of being a success?"

I have broken down the answer to this question into five significant factors: collaboration, relationships, ambition, passion, and persistence. In doing so, I aim to turn the crap that is fed to you by the Luddites and scaremongers into the CRAPP that can help you to ignore that negativity and go forward, undaunted, to carve out a successful life for yourself, earning a good living through the work you were born to do.

IT HAS NEVER BEEN EASY

During the decades I have spent making music, it has never been easy. Some things were easier in my first twenty years: first, having an album go platinum; doing a basic song demo (piano, guitar, and vocals) and having an artist listen to and record it, and second, getting paid by a club owner for performing. But read *easier,* not *easy.* Nowadays, some things are easier still—you might even say easy, such as getting a platform for your recorded work (websites and social media); laying down tracks (digital recording); and giving yourself a chance to be seen (YouTube).

However, the elements I describe in CRAPP have always been needed to maximize one's chances for success.

I emphasize collaboration and relationships, because I have found that the importance of these elements in creating a career is often undervalued. I also pay special attention to ambition because of the tendency of some young people I have mentored to think of ambition as a negative asset associated with being pushy, cutthroat, and selfish—a perspective that results in a laissez-faire attitude to the proactive approach needed for a chance at a successful career.

"My talent and the great work I do should be enough to achieve my goals" is a statement I have heard. If your goal is to create something you think is wonderful, and you take satisfaction in that without desiring more, i.e., a career, then amen. Stay in your comfort zone, and let the world somehow come to you. It might. However, the world is filled with talented people striving to be successful and using every legitimate tool at their disposal to attain that success. The world is not waiting for them or you, but they are working hard to make the world notice them and their talent.

We are all unique beings who believe our talents deserve to be acknowledged and rewarded. Believing that you deserve success is good if it motivates you but not so good if you believe that deserving it means you will get it. Repeat after me: deserve's got nothing to do with it.

The young artists I mentor, who perform their own material,

often see cowriting a song, particularly the lyrics, as a weakness—as not having what it takes to do it on your own. This attitude has been formed by the belief that if the words you sing are not yours, then you are not legitimate. Perhaps this is a product of paying too much attention to social media, where everyone is a critic. Some are vehement in their belief that artists should write their own lyrics.

This is especially true in rap, where credibility, or "street cred," is always an issue with the cognoscenti. Writing about your life experience in your own words seems to be the key to that credibility. Everyone has the right to be a critic, and everyone now has the means to put it out into the world. My aim is to impart my belief that the end result—the power of the work—is what matters.

Collaborating on a lyric, could create a more potent lyric. Your role as the artist is to deliver those words with conviction and strength. Interpreting a lyric is equally as important as the words you sing. Write your own lyric if that is what your muse tells you to do, but do not feel that you are less than if you have given your own inimitable interpretation to someone else's lyrics.

It seems that writing your own words, telling your story, and opening up the events of your emotional life has become an expectation of an artist's audience. Outrage appears in social media if the perception is that the story is not sung in the artist's own words. The artist might then be called inauthentic, but in far more condemning language.

Young artists who have grown up with social media can become sensitive to this type of reaction, and this point of view can become part of their own belief systems. As a result, they may feel that they are being artistically weak by collaborating on lyrics or singing words to their songs written by another writer. I have often walked delicately around this issue when collaborating with an artist who has this perspective and who is often an excellent lyricist.

I have also encountered artists who are far more comfortable writing music and melodies but feel pressure to write their own lyrics. In these cases, it is easier for me to have my ideas accepted. But in both scenarios, it is incumbent upon me to make artists feel secure that I am there to help them express their stories and their world views. I am not a usurper; I am an ally.

My approach often results in long conversations with artists about their lives and beliefs so that I can empathize with the raison d'être for their songs. Communication is the key to developing a comfort zone between collaborators. A few hours of talking and a solid half hour of writing is my favorite kind of session.

Hopefully I have unencumbered my collaborators of the idea that they are weak or inauthentic artists because they have allowed others to contribute to their songs.

Elton John often sang words written by Bernie Taupin. Adele recorded a unique version of Bob Dylan's "Make You Feel My Love." Florence Welch reimagined Robert Palmer's "Addicted to Love." Joe Cocker reinvented The Beatles' "A Little Help from My Friends." Joni Mitchell, who is revered for her unique lyrics, sang "How Do You Stop," written by Charlie Midnight and Dan Hartman, with lyrics by Charlie Midnight. Many respected and well-known artists have sung my lyrics without being diminished or taken to task. The bottom line is to sing what you feel, regardless of who wrote the words with you or without you.

For songwriters who are not the artists, and for artists who care only about the quality of the songs, collaboration is an accepted and welcome practice. Collaboration in all fields is the norm, not the exception. You learn and grow from the cross-pollination of ideas, and it is essential to keep learning and growing. Knowledge is the fertile soil that grows the seeds of your next idea.

Forming and keeping relationships that could be beneficial to your career can be viewed as cynical calculations and self-serving manipulations that are unworthy of your higher intentions. Admitting that you are ambitious might be perceived as you wanting to succeed regardless of what you have to do to get there. Wanting to achieve something significant is a worthy objective that takes positive energy and intense ambition. Your drive must be stronger than your self-doubt. But your ethics and humanity do not need to be sacrificed in pursuit of your goal. Do you want the brass ring so badly that you feel justified in doing whatever it takes, regardless of the immoral consequences of your actions? Are you able to intellectually detach yourself from your basic humanity and decency in order to get what you want?

Ambition is often cast in a negative light and then studiously avoided by those people who do not want to cast aspersions on themselves. I want to unburden you of those attitudes that could be holding you back from achieving success. I want you to see that needing to collaborate does not lessen your own worthiness, rather it is a positive development when you make an honest connection with someone that is beneficial to your career. And I also want you to recognize that ambition is merely a strong drive for success that will not necessarily overpower all your goodness and cause you to lose your soul to the devil.

You cannot separate how you achieve something from the achievement. The sum of your accomplishments includes the means by which you get there. And the shortcuts might lead you nowhere and leave you stranded and lost in the desert of your own avarice.

There are no easy routes to attaining something of value. But you can, through your ambition, passion, persistence, and talent, reach the end for which you strive without sacrificing your integrity. You have the power to control your integrity. But success is dependent upon different factors that can come and go, and if it goes, then what you are left with is the state of your integrity and your conscience.

My integrity was in a questionable state, and my conscience was in an unconvincing state of denial when I fired my bass player in the midst of recording my album. We were ensconced in Newtown, Connecticut, in a recording studio in a woodsy location far from the eyes and ears of the record company. This might have been a good thing if I had known anything about recording at the time and, after slogging it out for so many years, did not feel so desperate to have a success.

The process of recording intimidated me, and as confident as I was performing onstage, I was equally unconfident singing in the studio. I relied on my producer to reassure me about my vocals and to point the recording in all the right directions. It is always a mistake for you to concede all control to a perceived savior. Ultimately, you should be the captain of your own ship, bearing the responsibility for the direction and final destiny of your work. The right collaborators will help you get there, but if you give up all your power out of fear, insecurity, exhaustion, or simple laziness, then you have no right to complain when you end up far from your destination.

I gave up my power, and the result was light years from what

I had envisioned. Still, I put my faith in those who I believed knew better than me. My overriding desire, regardless of my satisfaction with the final product, was to have a hit album and end my years of struggling.

In the middle of recording, my producer and the engineer pulled me aside for a serious conversation about their feeling that the bass player was not cutting it and needed to be replaced. The bass player had been in the band since its formation, and although it was contractually my band, each member had been a loyal and intimate part of the struggle. I had the legal right to fire him, but did I have the moral right to do so?

They insisted that it had to be done. In retrospect, it did not have to be done. If I had been versed in the mechanics of the recording process, I would have known that bands with less-than-stellar musicianship have recorded many successful albums through technical wizardry, ghost players brought in under the cover of night to replace parts, or time and energy spent with the band member to get it right. "We have to do what's right for the album," I was told.

In my desperation, exhaustion, insecurity, and lack of knowledge, I expediently ignored the intense clawing in my stomach and the choking pounding in my chest and fired the bass player. My integrity was hiding in some dark shadow, conveniently out of my sight, where it could not weigh in on my decision.

The bass player did not put up a fight, but the pain in his eyes and resignation in his voice almost weakened my resolve. He left the studio, and I have not since that moment heard or known anything about his life. And then with another bass player, who might or might not have been better for the music, the album did not succeed.

If the album had been successful, would my attitude about the immutable importance of keeping your integrity have been different? When I was on tour with the band, still thinking that there was a chance for the album to succeed, my conscience never stopped nagging at me. I had thoughts about asking the bass player to rejoin the band once the album was a hit. Would I have done it?

The recording studio was on a large piece of property owned by a man who would place mash on the ground not far from the studio and lie in wait for a hungry deer to approach. When the deer began to chomp on the food, he would kill the animal. One day the man came to the studio and asked us to help him drag the warm carcass to the barn. At first I felt uneasy grabbing onto the limb of the freshly dead animal and pulling it across the cold, snowy ground. But in minutes the unease subsided. I had helped out a neighbor, and he invited us to join him in the evening for a venison dinner.

There was a purpose to that killing: dinner. My discomfort was in having to touch the warm dead body. Once I got used to that, which I did quickly, I had no second thoughts about the matter. There was an absolute, explicit purpose to what had occurred. If you believe in eating meat, then there is no moral ambiguity—no crisis of conscience.

When I think about those days in Connecticut recording the album, I have merged the firing of the bass player with the killing of the deer into some kind of parable. Both images play simultaneously in my memory. Killing the deer, as uncomfortable as it was for me, had a reason that I could easily justify with no damage to my integrity. I have never felt justified in letting the bass player go and believe that it was a stain on my integrity that would have made incomplete and unsatisfactory any success of the album.

You want to achieve success, but you also want to build a foundation for continued success. Your reputation for integrity is a critical element in laying that foundation. Success without integrity is a house of cards, vulnerable to any ill wind that may blow its way.

It is crap, spelled with one *P*, that you can't earn a good living in the music business. It is CRAPP, with two *P*s, that will give you the power and best chance to achieve that goal. Of course, there are other elements that might assist you on your journey: having a family member, preferably one or both of your parents, in an influential position in the line of work to which you aspire (even better if they own the company); or ridiculous luck. Sadly, most of us cannot count on these things. And even if you get through the door through these connections, you will not stay there without CRAPP.

Chapter Three
COLLABORATION

*In the long history of humankind (and animal
kind, too) those who learned to collaborate and
improvise most effectively have prevailed.*

CHARLES DARWIN

*If there is any one secret of success, it lies
in the ability to get the other person's point
of view and see things from that person's
angle as well as from your own.*

HENRY FORD

Being a good collaborator is a strong asset in any working relationship, regardless of the field in which you work. Collaboration is our first initial of CRAPP.

I have written songs in almost any way you can imagine and virtually all in collaborations with other writers. Being a good collaborator has been the cornerstone of my career as a songwriter and record producer. As a record producer, I have worked with artists as disparate as Joe Cocker and Hilary Duff, and I came to each project with the understanding that I had to develop a relationship based on trust and respect with the artist—two factors that form the foundation of any good collaboration.

Almost everyone in the music business today collaborates. That is the landscape. There are exceptions, but if you want to increase your chances of making a living, then you must have people wanting to collaborate with you.

Often, your skill set is partnered with another skill set, and this is called collaboration. This holds true whether you are a lyricist, a melodist (a "topliner" in current vernacular), or a person who does tracks. It is important to always remember that you are in a partnership and not doing a solo turn, and the aim of this partnership is to create a mutually beneficial and satisfying result.

Of course, your brilliance will lead people to want to collaborate with you, but it is somewhat important that they are comfortable with your personality and willingness to compromise and to be open minded. You can close many doors for yourself if, after you leave the session, the first thought of your collaborator is, "Good riddance." Such a reaction will definitely not be due to your talent, which we know is prodigious, and so it will most likely be caused by some friction between you and the other party, which is probably his or her fault, but maybe not. Or maybe there was no friction, and you went away thinking, "That went great." It is incumbent upon you, if you want to maximize your chances of a career, to be able to form and keep collaborations and to figure out how to do so.

One suggestion is don't shoot first and ask questions later. Take a deep breath before you react strongly against your collaborator's idea. Use your intellect and your words to then coherently explain your differing point of view. Accept the possibility that you might have to accede, and do so without rancor. You can be strong about your beliefs without being insulting, demeaning, or condescending—attitudes that might easily poison the atmosphere of any collaboration.

Once a good collaboration is established and ongoing, with all parties feel secure and respected in the relationship, then the dynamics might change, and you could possibly object to an idea by saying, "That sucks," or "You're not serious." However, at first, tread carefully.

It is different today than when I first started. There were no track guys and no topliners. There was a lyricist and a melodist (usually someone who played an instrument), and sometimes the same person covered both bases. Then there were arrangers, who would take the song and create an arrangement for a recording. Often, the person who created the melody and the music was also the arranger.

Sometimes, as happened with Dan Hartman and myself, the lyrics came first. Other times, the music and melody came first. Sometimes the melody and lyrics happened simultaneously. In bands, a member might come in with an idea for a song that the band would then expand upon, and the lead singer would be expected to write the lyrics and, often, the melody.

Bands, in the best cases, could raise collaboration to its highest level, where four or five or six people would be contributing ideas and finding ways to make it work. Great bands could often create beauty out of chaos and arrive in exotic places that classic songwriting collaborations would never visit. Again, it is all about collaboration.

Being effective means getting the result you want, and that means getting a great song out of the collaboration, or a great vocal out of a singer in a recording session, or creating a great track; it doesn't mean you getting your idea accepted regardless of whether it is the best idea. That is not constructive. Your idea might be the best idea, but let the other ideas in; try them. In a good collaboration, it will sort itself out. The cream will rise to the top, but only if all collaborators are open minded and respectful of each other and understand that the only result that will benefit everyone in the situation is a great product.

I have collaborated and had success in a variety of genres because I have learned to first earn my collaborators' trust and respect by giving them my respect and trust. Although my ideas are usually the best, it is up to me to accept that my collaborators might also have some acceptable ideas. So the question is, why collaborate if you can do it all by yourself? It is not necessarily a question of a result being better or worse but, rather, of being *different*; something you would not have come up with unilaterally that expands your own possibilities.

It has been beneficial for me to be versatile and work successfully in different genres. But being able to move comfortably among different styles is an asset, not a necessity, and being perceived as great at what you do and as a desired collaborator is enough to form the foundation of your continued success. If you have the ability and the inclination, however, then being versatile and adapting to different situations will increase your chances for success and longevity. The best results I have had as a record producer have been on the occasions when I set an atmosphere in which everyone feels comfortable contributing their ideas.

There are many people who have enjoyed great success in one specific genre—that seems to be the norm. For me, though, being versatile has helped me survive the vagaries of the life I chose and thrive in the job I love. Being adaptable to many styles while being equally inspired in each of them could widen the career possibilities for you, too. Even if you already have a successful career in one genre, crossing over into another might open the door to new successes and creative satisfactions.

I began my career in bands, writing songs for myself. When my artist career crashed and I was given jobs writing for and working with artists of various styles, I was forced to understand and immerse myself in each genre, respecting the artist and valuing the opportunity. I was grateful to be working and wanted to keep working. Wanting to keep working using my talent was the catalyst for my versatility. I do not judge whether one genre is more worthy than another. My goal, regardless of the style of music or my personal taste, is to do a great job.

I produced an album for Joe Cocker called *Unchain My Heart*, for which we recorded a version of the title song, written by Bobby Sharp and originally recorded by Ray Charles. Michael Lang, Joe's manager at the time, had suggested doing the song, and the thought of it was daunting. It was hard to imagine improving on a classic recording by the iconic and incomparable Ray Charles, who was also Joe Cocker's main influence and idol.

Before recording the song, we rehearsed it in a rehearsal studio. Joe's input was essential to ensure that he would be inspired by the arrangement and that it would be true to his own inimitable style. We were able to create a distinct version of the song as a result of the ideas flowing freely from all the collaborators in the room. When producing a song, I view all the essential participants as collaborators: artists, musicians, engineers, and whoever else is present and might have a laudable thought.

When we were in the recording studio working on the song, the band was nailing it. The track was as perfect as we had rehearsed it, but it was not satisfying me. I felt that we needed a signature introduction, a piece of music that would identify the song within its first seconds. My thought went out to the band, and Jeff Levine, the piano player, came up with the indelible cascading piano part for the song's intro that heralded Joe Cocker's rendition of "Unchain My Heart." Create a fertile environment for collaboration, and the creativity will flourish, and great ideas will grow.

With the right collaborator, it is an enjoyable process, a fine way to spend a few hours working at something that does not feel like work. If you cannot be a good collaborator, then be lucky. Lefty Gomez, the great New York Yankees pitcher, said, "I'd rather be lucky than good." So maybe you're the lucky one; but you can't count on that. Most of the time, you've got to be both lucky and good—a good collaborator.

That is not to say that you can't be successful without collaborations, but trust me—as my mother Bella used to say, "It can't hurt."

DAN HARTMAN

My most important collaboration and friendship in the course of my career was with a musical genius named Dan Hartman, who was one the few people who thought highly of the Charlie Midnight album, although, admittedly, he too did not buy it. A friend who had worked for the record company had sent my album to him, and he loved it.

More to the point, he loved my lyrics and wanted to meet me to talk about collaborating on some songs. Because even I did not love my album, Dan's reaction was quite surprising, but it was the beginning of my understanding of the importance and power of being a good collaborator.

Dan called me, and we arranged a meeting at a coffee shop on Fifty-Seventh Street and Broadway, where he told me that he was a fan of my lyrics and that he was looking to partner with a lyricist. I had possessed no knowledge of Dan Hartman's achievements until various people who were very excited about this development educated me. I researched Dan's history old-school style (pre-Google) by buying his albums and perusing the credits. Dan had been successful writing his own lyrics, and I asked, at our first writing session, why he felt that he needed a collaborator, having had such good results on his own. In retrospect, he could have said, "Good question. Why fix what isn't broke? Let me show you to the door." Instead, to my good fortune, he answered, "I don't need it. I want it. I'm evolving." I am sure that recollection is accurate, because it affected and helped me to define the way I would continue thereafter with my own career and life. Our initial conversation at the coffee shop went something like this:

Dan: I'm looking for a writing partner.

Charlie: Considering I'm broke, working the graveyard shift as a legal proofreader, and I've been dropped from the label. Let's go for it.

The result was that, together, we wrote for artists such as

James Brown ("Living in America"), Joni Mitchell ("How Do You Stop"), Billy Joel ("Why Should I Worry" from *Oliver and Company*), and Teenage Mutant Ninja Turtles ("9.95").

Perhaps Dan's most popular song as an artist was the song "I Can Dream About You," from the film *Streets of Fire*. He also sang and wrote the rock-and-roll classic "Free Ride" and the disco evergreens "Relight My Fire" and "Instant Replay." He produced much of Tina Turner's *Foreign Affair* album, including the iconic song "The Best," which was written by the songwriting legends Mike Chapman and Holly Knight.

My collaboration with Dan began in 1983, and almost immediately we had some success—my first success—with a song called "Heart of the Beat," featured in the film *Breakin'*. The film was a low-budget affair featuring hip-hop music, a form that was fast becoming popular. Nobody wanted to write for it, because its chances for success seemed slim to none, and there was almost no budget for licenses. So the music supervisor, who knew Dan, called and asked him to write a song. I was still working the graveyard shift as a legal proofreader at a law firm on Wall Street.

Dan wasn't that interested, because the license fee was only—*only*—$5,000. I needed the money. Dan didn't. His challenge to me was that if I had a lyric finished by five o'clock in the evening, then he would write the music. It was already one o'clock. Of course, I finished the lyrics with time to spare. As promised, Dan wrote the music. The music supervisor loved it.

Happy ending? Not yet.

The song we first wrote for the film was called "We Are the Young." At the time, Dan was about to record his own album, and his label heard the song and insisted that Dan keep it for himself. Dan informed the music supervisor of this, who, of course, became angry, because they had already shot a major scene in the film to the song. Dan offered to write another, and we did: "Heart of the Beat." By the time Dan submitted the song, the music supervisor had commissioned another writing team, Ollie and Jerry, to write and record a song with the exact same beat and tempo for the scene in the movie that had been shot. It was a fait accompli.

Nevertheless, our song would be used in the film but not in the major dance number. Another problem arose when we could not get an artist to perform the song. Dan had an idea that he and I would sing it under a pseudonym. Thus, we became the hip-hop group called 3V, a name with no significance but much mystique. I got my $2,500, and the album went on to sell three million copies. I was finally, for the first and last time, a hit artist.

Subsequently, a concert promoter looking to book 3V for spring break in Fort Lauderdale contacted Dan. We went and sang "Heart of the Beat" on the beach for thousands of kids, and we did it to a track—no band. It was the easiest gig I ever played, and the last.

That is the story of my first success. There is, however, an epilogue.

The song "We Are the Young," which the label insisted Dan keep for himself, made it to number twenty-five on the singles charts. Good, but less than expected. The song "No Stoppin' Us," by Ollie and Jerry, which replaced "We Are the Young" in the surprise hit movie *Breakin'* and was the single from the surprise hit soundtrack album, made it to number one on the singles charts. Would "We Are the Young" have gone to number one if it had been the single from the film? Maybe yes, but then

3V would not have had its day in the sun. I have no regrets. My cup runneth over.

Sometimes your biggest disappointments can become your biggest blessings. While I did not experience the electricity of having a number-one song—and it is presumptuous to think that the film alone would have made a difference—I was finally a singer on a hit album, which, with some creative logic, made me a hit artist. Over the years, I have told that story many times with great relish, and I always get a great response. I have turned a negative into a positive. Time and distance can do that.

Curiously, I have from time to time encountered ardent fans of the film *Breakin'* who are thrilled to meet 3V and who then sing to me the chorus of the song and ask for autographs, which I proudly and eagerly sign "3V, Keep Breakin'."

My career has been, as most are (as I previously mentioned), a zigzagging, circuitous, unmarked road leading to where I am now. It seems to be the same case for most people I have talked to. You go here, and you go there; you walk through this door and that door; you fall off cliffs, climb up hills, and get stuck in the mud; and then, if you survive the journey, some guardian angel pulls you out of the muck when you least expect it, just when you have resigned yourself to being okay with whatever fate the universe has assigned you, no matter how ignominious or how many light years away you are from where you once dreamed you would be.

When I started my partnership with Dan Hartman, I had had little experience in the delicate dynamics needed for collaborations outside of bands. Band disagreements could have ended in members storming out of rehearsal. A physical confrontation had always been a possibility, but, assuming the conflict had not broken up the band, there was always the next rehearsal to work it out. Everyone had a personal and vested interest in the music and keeping the band together; it had not been a context for developing our diplomatic skills.

Outside the universe of bands, it is important to be a diplomat in the pursuit of getting your point across and to have the willingness to keep an open mind. Working with Dan was like going to an institute of higher learning in pursuit of a PhD in the art of collaboration. Before this, I had been the lead singer in bands and expected to write the lyrics, and it had been expected for those lyrics to express my experience and worldview. That had been my job, and, for the most part, no collaboration had been necessary. If I had received any input from other band members, I could have accepted it or rejected it. I had been the arbiter.

When the band had been working out the music, strong viewpoints and opinions came from all directions. This was often a rough-and-tumble kind of collaboration, a test of wills and convictions. When the dust had settled, the band, bloodied but unbroken, had worked out the music in question. We never needed to be concerned about establishing a relationship, because the band *was* the relationship. I learned nothing from my days in bands about the art of diplomacy and the need to form business and creative relationships. My goal had been to be the singer in a successful rock group, and I was very experienced in that kind of collaboration.

Now I was working with Dan Hartman, an exacting partner who demanded that he also be satisfied with the lyrics, and this meant often rewriting, carving, and changing words and then changing them back again. I could not be the sole arbiter of the lyrics or engage Dan in a brawl of ideas, hoping to be the last man standing. I learned to argue my opinion using as much logic as I could muster. Dan's reaction was often visceral and immediate—instinctive. A fearless communication evolved that was based on respect and the belief in the uniqueness of our collaboration.

Which opinion was better or worse did not enter into the dynamic, because we both understood that our sensibilities were not the same, and that, left alone, either of our opinions might or might not have worked, but the point of the collaboration was to create a work that was Hartman and Midnight, not Hartman alone or Midnight alone. A great collaboration is the coming together of two distinct, singular entities to create a new distinct, singular entity. If that is not the point, then why have a collaboration? Why not just go solo?

However, I did develop a method of avoiding the discomfort of having to rewrite what I usually considered to be brilliant lyrics. I came to realize that if I gave my esteemed colleague choices of many different lyrics for the same song, he took pleasure and was satisfied in choosing what he thought were the best ones. Consequently, I started handing in pages of lyrics without caring about which ones he chose, because I considered them all to be brilliant. Dan did not always share that opinion, but he always found something there that he liked and even loved.

I enjoy overwriting, because I can often see many different alternatives and take pleasure in working them all to fruition. It is even more pleasurable when I get to write the lyrics before the music is composed. That was the way Dan liked to work, and it is still my favorite way of working. It allows me more latitude in the words I choose, because I am not restricted to a melody that supposes a particular syllabic pattern. Still, I have been in countless collaborations where the melody is written first, and my challenge is to fit lyrics into that melody. The latter is the more common method of songwriting, which I also love, especially when the melody is inspiring. A great melody, classically, trumps all. Combine that with great lyrics, and you might have a song for the ages. That does not necessarily mean that the song will be a hit, because commercial success is a phenomenon resulting from a convergence of many factors. It's also measurable and objective, as is the success of making a living with your talent, which might not include having a hit song but would be a commercial business that earns you money.

Artistic success is subjective and often changes with the zeitgeist of the times. Works that were at first artistically unheralded are revisited one day and become artistically lauded. Commercial and artistic success are not mutually exclusive, although *commercial* is often seen as having a negative connotation equivalent to *selling out*. I understand people who want to protect what they consider the purity of artistic expression, but having a commercial success does not mean the artist has sold out. It means the artist has been able to successfully sell his or her work.

The idea that artists might be selling out, especially to young idealists, can be confusing and a product of peer pressure and paying too much attention to the negativists that troll social media. Using your talent to make a living is the goal. Follow your inspiration in whatever form it takes, and let it lead you to success in whatever form that takes. Control what you can, and do not get stymied by what is out of your control. You have power over what you create, keeping your passion and ambition alive, building relationships, and persisting until you arrive at your success. Do not get distracted by that over which you have no power, particularly whether your work is artistically successful. Just do the work.

There are many songs that are hits in the minds and hearts of the writers, artists, and their families and friends; coffee shop audiences; and people stopping on the street to listen to buskers—songs that are never released by labels or find large audiences. There are thousands (even millions) more that lie dormant in the files and archives of the creators and performers, to be heard and appreciated by a fortunate audience in homes, clubs, subway corridors, and the ubiquitous and democratizing internet.

A hit song is typically an anomalous product of corporate merchandising and audience acceptance, but a song that evokes an emotion in a listener—that creates an indelible and positive impression, whatever that may be to whatever audience—is a universal and common phenomenon in every culture, because I believe that music and song are written in the genetic code, or, at least, have evolved as a necessity for our survival. I write this as a layman on instinct and as part of the collective consciousness and not as a scientist: human beings need music, but not the music business. But if you have a big commercial success, be humble in the face of all the elements that had to converge for you to achieve that success.

You should be so lucky.

BELLA KAUFMAN, NEE HANFT (1918–2012)

We who seek to earn a living through our passions and talents need to make some kind of business out of the work or play that inspires us. Being able to collaborate successfully is one element that helps us to reach that goal and can easily be applied to any field of work for anyone seeking to earn a living doing what he or she loves to do.

THE CHARLIE MIDNIGHT BAND AND THE ROAD TO A RECORD DEAL

My experience in the Charlie Midnight Band (*Innocent Bystander*, Decent Records/Columbia, 1982) was a variation of the kind of band dynamics that I described. It was never my dream to write songs for other artists; I had my own statements to make as a performer.

I had left the Brooklyn bar circuit, where I had sung only cover songs, so that I could write and sing my own words and stories. As a professional songwriter seeking to get your songs covered by recording artists, you are writing for those artists, trying to anticipate, to some degree, what they would want to sing. As a band member writing songs for the band, you only have to be concerned with satisfying yourself and your fellow band members. It is a different kind of collaboration, and I was unprepared for the type of songwriting collaboration that would soon, fortuitously, be thrust upon me by my guardian angel, Dan Hartman.

Before we got our record deal, the Charlie Midnight Band played a few gigs after rehearsing for many months and had packed Max's, Kansas City. The Max's show was a triumph, and after the show, an attorney approached me. He was excited about what he had heard and seen and asked me if I had a demo. "I don't give demos to attorneys," I answered, and walked away, doing my best antiestablishment strut.

My "I don't give a damn" attitude had been honed by many years of near misses, too many bad gigs, and too many great gigs that paid almost nothing and led nowhere but back to the rehearsal studio. Not giving a damn set me free, or as Bob Dylan sang, "When you got nothing, you got nothing to lose." The freedom I felt was the freedom from expectations. The years of struggling had taken a toll, and I had to make peace with where I was in my journey, which was not where I had expected to be at that juncture in my life.

It is a revelation to value a beautiful moment so highly that it becomes your raison d'être. Put enough of those beautiful moments together, and you have lived a beautiful life. So I said what I said to the attorney, because I did not want go back to that place of expectations. I was at peace with the time and place and was exhilarated from the band's great performance. That moment was enough.

At our next performance at Max's, the attorney brought with him a man from the record company to see our show. We were not forewarned and so could not blame being nervous for our clamorous, teetering performance. I was unnerved by the band's descent into klutziness, and it eroded my own rock-and-roll bravado.

The bass player had hurt his thumb prior to the show, and his playing was erratic, less driving, and often out of sync with the drummer. Because drums and bass are the foundation of most songs, and our songs were particularly dependent on those instruments locking together in a tight rhythm, the other players in the band, myself included, had overcompensated by playing too loud and singing too hard. In the course of the set, I became self-conscious, thinking that the audience could perceive these gaffes. The gig felt like an out-of-control semitruck careening down a steep incline toward oblivion.

Immediately after coming off the stage, the bass player came up to me and apologized. He was distraught. We were all distraught as we moped into the dressing room. After a few minutes, the attorney entered the room with the record executive and introduced himself and the exec, who said, "Great show, guys," and then leaned over to me and whispered, "I love the bass player. Great chops."

The next day, I had a meeting with the record executive, and he offered the band a record deal, which, still in my "don't give a damn" pose, I did not digest until, as I was about to leave, he asked, "So what about it?"

"What about what?" I asked.

"I'm offering the band a record deal," he replied. As he opened the door for me and I walked slowly past him into the corridor, I said indifferently, "Really? I'll talk to the band."

I offer that as an example of how you should not begin a collaboration or, foreshadowing the next chapter, a relationship. I might have said, sounding needful and uncool but honest, "Thank you. This is what I have worked toward for so many years, pushing through the hurt, the rejection, the depression, and the resignation." He would have appreciated my openness and lack of pretension. I might have said, with equal honesty but with less neediness, while maintaining my street aplomb, "Thanks, man, solid—that's great. Let me talk to the band and hit you right back." Either remark would have been a good beginning to a working relationship. I am sure that you can think of many more that would have set the right tone. Instead, I pulled the "I don't give a damn" armor tightly around my ego, and when I left the building and started walking numbly toward nowhere, I thought to myself, "You schmuck. Maybe you blew it." Strangely, I did not blow it, and after talking to the band, I called the record guy and said, "Yeah, why not."

It is hard to prevent years of constant frustration from festering until you become infected with bitterness and cynicism. At the point where I was being offered a record deal, I had already resigned myself to the fact that I might never reach that goal. It was my need to keep creating and the satisfaction I got from writing a song and having a good gig that pushed me onward. I was focused on the moment and not on where the moment might lead. Having no expectations gave me a sense of peace. I was comfortable with that state of mind. As I sat across from the record guy, I felt that sense of peace being disturbed and reflexively wanted to douse that unsettling flicker of hope. However, luck was with me that day.

In spite of what I considered a misguided start to my collaboration and relationship with the record company, it seems they were not turned off, and we made the record. I credit that to serendipity. The other factors at work would obviously be persistence and passion, without which there would not have been, after so many years of slogging it out, a Charlie Midnight Band.

My cynical rebel stance was a shield against my anticipation of the next rejection, the inevitable hurt that I had come to expect. But it could have been the open manhole into which I fell, free falling to my demise because I was not paying attention to where I was going. It is not insane or unintelligent to become disenchanted and pessimistic in a world that wreaks havoc on your body, soul, and dreams. But it is crazy to let it take you over and suppress your idealism to the extent where you cavalierly kick away opportunity and hope. Let your idealism suppress your cynicism. Idealism is a much more powerful force than cynicism. It can change the world; it *has* changed the world.

> *A cynic is a man who, when he smells*
> *flowers, looks around for a coffin.*
>
> **H. L. MENCKEN**

ROAD TO A RECORD DEAL

I had formed yet another band. Persistence, passion, and thickheadedness were the traits that sustained me. There was a new label called Decent Records looking to sign a rock band. We were a rock band. The attorney for the label saw the band at Max's and reacted favorably. I was rude to him, but he was undeterred and brought the head of the label to our next show. In the next show, our bass player performed with a broken thumb. His crippled playing threw the band into an insecure spin, and the show was a mess of mistakes. The record guy was impressed with the bass player, who had compensated for his lameness by wildly jumping around onstage dressed in a tuxedo. I went to meet the record guy at his office, although I wanted to blow off the meeting in solidarity with my antiestablishment posture. The record guy, who had been a successful rock drummer, was not turned off by my "too-cool-for-the-room" affectation. Perhaps he was drawn to it, but I never asked. We were offered a record deal.

There are those chosen few to whom serendipity brings quick and effortless success and who believe that their success is a preordained certainty. Allowing that anything is possible in an unknowable universe, perhaps that belief is not ridiculous, self-serving, and egocentric. Alas, those of us hoi polloi who have not yet been visited by Lady Luck may need an alternative plan that includes, but is not limited to, being a good and thus sought after collaborator.

Don't waste too much time trying to figure it out. Just do it, and do it, and do it until you stop for a breath and think, "I don't know how I got here, but here I am, and I like this place." Nobody really knows anything, and the realization of that fact does not mean that you should not have an opinion or that you should not be open to outside ideas or advice. It is important to keep an open mind and take in other people's opinions that have resulted from their experiences. It is also important to know that they are only opinions, and that it is paramount that you have your own idiosyncratic vision. You take in what strikes the right chord and reject what feels wrong, but *keep an open mind.*

MASTER P, LIL' ROMEO

Chico Bennett and I were producing a song that we had written for Hilary Duff, a scheduled duet with Romeo Miller, known at the time as Lil' Romeo. Hilary would sing, and Romeo would rap. I wrote a lyric and a rap, and Chico and I were waiting in the studio with Hilary for Romeo's arrival. As we waited and waited and waited—approximately an hour and a half—I reviewed the rap many times and was very pleased with my work. It was not as if I had never before written a rap. In the halcyon days of singing in various bands, I would often tell a story in rhyme over a pulsating rhythm, very much in the style of Lou Reed's inspired "Walk on the Wild Side," which I consider one of the great all-time raps, or even the emotional rap in the song "Cry Baby," by Garnet Mimms and the Enchanters.

> *I've spent so many nights just waiting for you to come walking through the door. And even though you've made a fool of me so many times before, I know that all it takes is just the smile on your face to make me realize—that I'll always love you, darlin.'*
>
> *And I can see that you have more tears to shed. I can see it, baby, because your eyes, your eyes are getting red.*
>
> *So come on, come on, come on...and...Cry, Cry, Baby.*

On my album, *Innocent Bystander*, on the song of the same name, I had a slightly more frenzied rap over a drum and conga breakdown.

The lyrics were drawn from a fight between a collaborator of mine and a standard-issue Coney Island tough guy over a young woman on one hot summer night on the boardwalk in Brighton Beach, Brooklyn. Being a good collaborator, I felt it was my responsibility to support my friend, to have his back, and I jumped into the brawl. I survived the incident without remembering too many details other than the fact that many other toughs had joined the fracas and that I was conscious of trying to avoid my head being bashed in.

At some point, police sirens began wailing. Then someone pulled me out of the mess, and I found myself mysteriously back at my apartment, sans my leather vest and one of my motorcycle boots, and I thought, "I'm a rock-and-roll singer, an artist, and should be an observer and chronicler of, not a participant in, these types of altercations."

Days later, after hearing that some of the parties involved in the scrape were after me, I packed my things, moved to the city, and never looked back. "The city" was what we Brooklynites called Manhattan. Even today, for me, Manhattan is New York City, and the boroughs are the boroughs.

This particular type of collaboration made it hard enough to survive your life, let alone the hard knocks incurred when pursuing your dream, and it was essential only to my decision to get it together and focus on the end game: my music. My collaboration with my boardwalk tag-team partner effectively ended after that episode. He remained in Brooklyn. I hurried across the East River toward the next phase of whatever.

The following are a few of the words of the rap I wrote, which were inspired by that night, rather than a faithful retelling of reality. It begins:

> *Dancing in the shadows of the Boardwalk,*
> *trash can fire, flesh is hot.*
>
> *Renegade children with moonstruck eyes*
> *come to show you what they got.*

And ends:

> *Then Jackie sprung his switchblade but never had a chance,*
> *and everything went silent as he did his final dance.*
>
> *Then I heard his mama call, "Jackie boy, come home."*
>
> *And it echoed through the alleys where*
> *he'd carved his name in stone.*

Names were changed to protect those who were not so innocent, and as far as I know, no one died. It was, in retrospect, a little melodramatic for the recording, but when we performed it at shows, and I got down on my knees, falling onto the stage and writhing in tribute to Jackie's swan song, it was, when the audience was engaged, a very effective and chilling moment.

In writing the spoken words to "Innocent Bystander," I had prepared myself for the task of writing the rap for Romeo. When he finally arrived at the studio with an entourage and his father, the rapper Master P, I was confident about what I had written. Master P, of course, reviewed the rap and said something like, "This is good. Do you mind if I twist it a little?"

"Go ahead," I answered in the collaborative spirit.

By this time, after all my years of cowrites and taking input from artists and A&R people, I had learned to take a deep breath and step away from my preconceptions and my attachment to my words, which were often forged by hours of a painstaking, sometimes agonizing, search for the exact word or phrase or exact (or inexact) rhyme.

Master P finished twisting my rap in a fairly short amount of time and presented it to me as a matter of protocol and not, I believe, because he wanted my seal of approval. Following protocol can be paramount in collaborations, particularly when the relationship is new. As I reviewed Master P's rewritten version of my rap, I tried hard to recognize in his version a trace of my own. There was none. He had twisted and twisted until it was not even unrecognizable; it was a completely different rap, and better. No problem. Better is better.

ROCKY IV

The music supervisor for *Rocky IV* was a fan of Dan Hartman's and contacted Dan to write the song for the big fight
scene between the towering Russian and Rocky. I was Dan's
writing partner, and because of that relationship, I had the
privilege of cowriting with him "Living in America," which
became Mr. Brown's second-highest-charting song. All this
goes to show that good relationships build bridges from one
opportunity to the next.

We were both living on the East Coast at the time, and we
were flown out to Los Angeles to meet Sylvester Stallone. When
we got to the movie set, Stallone came out to greet us dressed
in boxing shorts and a robe. We went into his trailer to discuss
the song, and as we talked about what he was looking for, I said,
perhaps a bit presumptuously, "I don't want to write a jingoistic
'rah-rah' America song." Stallone didn't flinch and said simply,
"I see things in black and white. You guys are the songwriters.
Do what feels right." He loved songwriters and was respectful of
them, which, as you might imagine, is not always the case. So I
went back to the hotel, sat by the pool, and wrote the lyrics in
an afternoon, visualizing an American landscape.

Smokestack, fatback, many miles of railroad track.

*All-night radio keeps on running through
your rock-and-roll soul.*

All-night diners keep you awake on black coffee and a hard roll.

When I met James Brown, he said to me, "Charlie, you wrote
my life." To this day, I have never eaten any fatback, but it rhymed

with smokestack. The first time we met James Brown was when he came to the studio to record the song. He swept in with an entourage, and it felt surrealistic. I had seen James Brown and the Famous Flames decades before at the Brooklyn Fox Theater on Flatbush Avenue. (It was a "Murray the K" presentation and ran for three days. Murray the K—for Kaufman—was a D.J. who was, at the time, more famous than many of the acts in the revues he put on at the Brooklyn Fox, including the Miracles, Wilson Pickett, Marvin Gaye, the Ronettes, Jackie Wilson, Chuck Jackson, Ben E. King—I saw them all and sometimes in the same show.) But when the Godfather of Soul walked into the studio, for a moment I felt like I did not belong, as if I had been mistakenly hired to perform at a Murray the K extravaganza without a song to sing. But Mr. Brown greeted me with a smile and a strong handshake, saying "You boys wrote me a great song," and I was back, belonging in the session with James Brown.

Although he was sent the demo of the song weeks before the recording, Mr. Brown had not learned the lyrics. So I was given large sheets of drawing paper to write out the lyrics with a Magic Marker in large block letters. My highest marks in grade school were always for penmanship, so I was up to the task. I went over the lyrics with Mr. Brown and then stayed in the studio, quietly moving the cue sheets as he sang. The words were spread on top of a baby grand piano, because the sheets were too large for a music stand. The studio session went smoothly. I stood at his side by the piano, and we went over the lyrics. Now it was all about getting an honest James Brown vocal, and Mr. Brown was the consummate professional, fully invested in infusing the song with his full-tilt, uncompromising soulfulness. Dan Hartman danced in the control room as James Brown kept pumping up the track with his explosive energy. When Dan made one of his very few suggestions about phrasing or delivery, Mr. Brown gave no pushback. There was an atmosphere of conciliation in the studio.

Once in a while, James Brown would stop and regale us with some stories. It felt like the recording session had become, in spite of the throng of spectators in the studio, an intimate hangout among James Brown and the boys who wrote the song. Although we could never be James Brown's peers, there was a professional and artistic respect among the three of us, an understanding that the priority was to serve the song.

When James Brown finished singing and we were about to close the session, Dan Hartman pressed the talk-back button on the recording console and, in a I-might-be-walking-on-thin-ice tone of voice, asked, "Mr. Brown, before we call it a wrap, would you mind doing one more thing? Would you mind singing 'I feel good' at the end of the song—an homage to your legacy?" James Brown obliged, and that was a wrap.

When Mr. Brown was finished singing, I shook his hand, and a cup of coffee that I was holding tipped slightly and spilled a few drops onto the sheet with the chorus lyrics. At first I was aghast, thinking that I had ruined this great memento that I was planning to take with me. Then I thought, "That's art," and had him sign the paper. He wrote, "Charlie Midnight, You've Got the Word. Thanks for the love. James Brown."

Rocky IV was released with three minutes of "Living in America" performed on screen by James Brown in a boxing ring—a star-spangled spectacle that shot our song up the charts.

After the success of *Rocky IV* and "Living in America," Dan and I were asked to write and produce an entire album for James

Brown. My collaboration and relationship with Dan Hartman, my ambition to achieve something, my passion for my chosen career, and my persistence in the pursuit of my dream were all critical elements in bringing me to a place where I was sharing the floor, standing side by side, with Soul Brother Number One as he sang the words I had written.

THE DOOBIE BROTHERS

Learning to be a good collaborator, being able to adjust to a style and a situation, has allowed me to have a wide variety of opportunities.

I cowrote with Eddie Schwartz and Tommy Johnston a hit song called "The Doctor" for the Doobie Brothers' *Cycles* album. Eddie and I also coproduced part of the album with the Doobies.

Tommy was not used to cowriting, and we were given a directive to write something that harkened back to the heyday of the Doobie Brothers. Tommy had written "Listen to the Music" and "Long Train Running," two classic songs. The Doobies had sold over forty million albums.

For reasons that you could attribute to hubris, the record company had decided that the band needed assistance in writing a hit. I believe that Tommy was not pleased with this, and to this day is not fond of the song. Nevertheless, we had a job to do, and Tommy was cooperative.

Before the album was released, I received a call from the executive in charge of the album telling me that he did not think that we had a single but that "The Doctor" was going to be the single, because they had to release something, and that one had echoes of the classic Doobie songs. I am usually not privy to the thought processes of the decision makers and often do not understand or agree with the decisions. Which song will be the single, whether there will be a single, whether the album will be released, or whether the artist will be dropped from the label (because, for some reason, the label has lost belief in the artist that they had signed with much fanfare) are all out of my control.

I never stop being disappointed by these occurrences, but I have learned to move on to the next song, the next project, and the next use of my creativity. You should never develop a skin so thick that you are numb to the disappointments. Let those disappointments fuel your determination to succeed and stoke the fires of your passion: passion can strengthen persistence and catalyze ambition.

This comment about not having a hit single on the album made by the A&R executive was disheartening. During the part of the production in which I was involved, we had received positive responses to the music, and there seemed to be much enthusiasm for "The Doctor." It was reminiscent of the glory days of the band. Why the change of heart by the label? To this day I have no idea, but the committee often makes these types of judgments, and it is possible that the committee had decided, after all the enthusiasm for "The Doctor," that there was no obvious single. But the song was a hit. It reached number four on the pop charts and was the last Doobie Brothers hit. As Bella might have said, "Naysayers, shmaysayers. Let them kish mine tokus."

In this collaboration, I had to be respectful of Tommy's history as a hit songwriter, as well as Eddie's ("Hit Me with Your Best Shot," sung by Pat Benatar). Each of us had had success as writers. The dynamics could have been ego driven, but we all moved carefully through the process, and there was little friction.

Eddie and I had collaborated previously, and that fact probably made the process even smoother.

Every new collaboration presents a new dynamic that you have to figure out. Never take it for granted. Go into the new collaboration with the same considerations of respect, open mindedness, and diplomacy, and the understanding that your end game is to make it work. If you make it work, you will have a product you are proud of. Be the diplomat in the room, the one who understands that the priority is the end product, and don't be the one pushing your ideas just because they are *your* ideas. Be smart.

The benefits of forming successful collaborations can be ongoing and fruitful. Leave each collaboration with your collaborator wanting to work with you again due to the excellence of your contribution and the goodwill you left behind.

The label did not ask Eddie and me back for the remainder of the album due to the intense friction that swirled around The Plant Recording Studio in Sausalito during production. It was deeply disappointing, as I felt that we were making great music and that my relationship with the band, which I had worked hard to maintain, was one of friendship and reciprocity.

I did not write again with Tommy, but I was asked a few years later to produce a live Doobie Brothers album at the Sony Soundstage in New York City. Since the band was very capable after all these years of producing it themselves, I assumed that I was hired because of the goodwill I left behind. This was especially rewarding in that I believed in my ability to create good relationships even in the throes of adversity—another relationship, another job.

I survived wrong choices and deep disappointments and

learned to trust myself to handle conflicts and create bonds. There was no watershed moment when I said to myself, "I have learned this lesson." My education was slow but steady. Each time I rebounded from a setback, I became a little stronger, a bit more confident, and a fraction more astute in the ways of survival and the intricate politics of successful collaborations. The point is that my being able to negotiate the often-rough waters of collaboration over so many years in so many different styles with so many different collaborators has allowed me, thirty years after my first success, to wake up every morning and look forward to going to work.

JOE COCKER

When the Charlie Midnight Band was touring for the *Innocent Bystander* album, we were fortunate to open a few shows for Joe Cocker, whom I had seen in my teenage years in concert with Mad Dogs and Englishmen. This performance was one of my inspirations for wanting to sing and to be a performer.

I was excited. It was one of the few positive experiences as we toured behind an album with dwindling support from the label and moribund album sales. Yet, these were our best shows, because Joe Cocker's audiences were freewheeling, nonjudgmental, and determined to have a good time. The best show was in Odessa, Texas, the oil town where the workers worked hard and played hard and loved us before we had plugged in the guitars. They cheered as the band tuned up as if they knew who we were. Our spirits were high, and I believe we played a great set. We all hung out in Joe's room after the show.

I had a feeling of hope and some elation as we went our

separate ways. Joe's band headed to its next headlining show, and we pushed on to a bar in Santa Fe. The owner was angry when we arrived, because the label refused to buy any radio ads in support of the gig. He told us to keep driving. Hope did not spring eternal. It lasted for the twelve hours it took us to get from Odessa to Santa Fe by way of dust storm that delayed our arrival by four hours.

After much pleading with the owner, we were allowed to play but without getting paid. Because the show went well, the owner fed us, and we feasted on some hamburgers and jumbo fries. Although the proverbial glass might truly have been as dry as the dust we had crawled through, I remember thinking that we had played two gigs in a row where our music had been well received. The cup looked, for a moment, to be at least half-full. I was able to live in the moment for the music and take satisfaction in a job well done, and to this day, the hamburgers still rate as the most delicious I have ever eaten.

Years later, when I was hired to produce a Joe Cocker album and Joe and I were again face to face, I told him that it was great to see him again. He obviously did not remember me and looked uncomfortable when I said "again," but he, being the gentleman that he was, pretended to be pleased to see me "again." That was the only uneasy part of our collaboration.

This was my first solo production, and I did not know what to expect from the legendary Joe Cocker who, with the Grease Band, had made an indelible mark at Woodstock with his definitive and transcendent rendition of "A Little Help from My Friends." Here was the artist who had been an inspiration to me, who I had successfully and enjoyably supported on my otherwise-fruitless and frustrating tour. The irony and implausibility of the scenario was not lost on me. I did not have much experience as a producer, and I was nervous.

The dynamics and protocol of your last collaboration may not be relevant to how you are going to solve the next one. Enter the situation carefully and respectfully but with the confidence that you are there because you are capable of doing the job. If part of the job is to collaborate, then make it a priority to create a good rapport and dynamic with your collaborator. Give respect, and you will get respect. Except for contributing his inimitable vocals, Joe had little involvement in his last few albums. I decided to insist that he be fully engaged in the process as the bandleader and in having a loud and deciding voice in choosing and arranging the songs. His artistic instincts were strong, and his participation in the whole process was vigorous and important to the success of the album.

Getting Joe to immerse himself in the creative process made the collaboration go smoothly. Trust was established between us, and trust is the bedrock of a successful collaboration.

Building trust with your collaborator requires you to listen closely to and respect the other person's ideas. It means that you make it clear at the outset that this is a collaboration of creative equals and that you are only interested in getting the best result. Ease into the collaboration, and be sensitive to the concerns of your collaborator.

When I am mentoring and collaborating with aspiring songwriters or artists, I always say, "You are the captain of your ship. I am the navigator, the guide who is here to help you reach your destination." I impress upon them that looking for a savior who will magically create their success will only stunt the growth of their unique visions, and it is their uniqueness that will win the day.

Being in an arena where the rules of conduct are undefined, you become wary when your power may appear to be threatened. It is important to understand that when you first enter this arena, your collaborator might feel protective. So, define the rules—cooperation, respect, and unselfishness—and establish that the purpose of the collaboration is to create something that satisfies both of you.

Trust will come in the doing, not simply the saying, but it is important to convey these beliefs to your collaborator to begin the process of gaining his or her trust. There is no exact road map to being trusted, but those rules are a good starting point. And then there is your own determination to establish a trust that sometimes might entail suppressing your emotions in order to advance your agenda: to get your collaborator to trust you. That trust will be the foundation of creating a work of which you are both proud and having a positive, pleasurable experience in the process.

The collaborative effort and the resulting relationship between Joe and me produced the album *Unchain My Heart*, which was an international hit. That led to us working together on the equally successful follow-up album, *One Night of Sin*. I had made it through a dust storm, a hamburger-paying job, and a record company that had abandoned me before my tour had ended and found myself, ridiculously, in a studio producing for and collaborating with an artist I idolized, who did not recall that we had once shared a stage. As Bella would say, "Go figure."

LAUREN CHRISTY

Lauren was born to be a songwriter and signed her first publishing deal at the age of seventeen. She is a natural pop songsmith who was a recording artist and subsequently has become a successful songwriter and record producer. With Lauren and her production team, comprising Scott Spock and Graham Edwards, aka "the Matrix," she produced and wrote "Complicated," the song that launched the career of Avril Lavigne. Together with the Matrix, I wrote "So Yesterday" for Hilary Duff.

Lauren and I began our collaboration before the Matrix was formed, when she was writing for her album *Breed*, which turned out to be her final solo-album. Lauren is an elegant, beautiful English woman whose talent seemed innate and to possess an easy flow, similar to Dan Hartman's. Lauren, like Dan, was to the "manner born."

Please do not confuse "to the manner born" with the phrase "to the *manor* born," which arose later in etymological history. I looked this up, because as I was writing the previous sentence, I questioned the accuracy of my usage. The phrase "to the manner born" appears in Shakespeare's *Hamlet,* Act 1, Scene 4:

> *Horatio: Is it a custom?*

> *Hamlet: Ay, marry, is't: But to my mind,*
> *though I am native here.*

> *And to the manner born, it is a custom More honoured*
> *in the breach than the observance.*

I care about the accuracy of words and phrases, because I care about language and the importance of being able to use it properly in expressing or explaining yourself and your position, which can be paramount in creating a successful collaboration.

Being skillful in the use of words heightens your ability to convey your message, your opinion, your enthusiasm, and your disappointment about any subject. Language aptitude fosters discussion and the sharing and expansion of ideas. It encourages other parties in the discussion or the collaboration to raise the level of their usage, and the result will be the cultivation of a richer collaboration. And a good communicator develops better relationships. There is no downside to having the facility to accurately impart your message and your feelings.

The difference between the right word
and the almost right word is the difference
between lightning and a lightning bug.

MARK TWAIN

With Lauren, I often wrote a lyric first. But she is also a fine lyricist, and as a result, I learned to be a stronger collaborator on lyrics. This speaks to the importance of understanding that there are often various ideas that can be good—in this case, lyrics for a song—and there should be mutual respect between collaborators and the open mindedness to take in your collaborator's ideas, digest them, and accept they might be equally or more appropriate than yours. In this instance, it might benefit the project and the cooperative spirit to use your collaborator's contribution. Of course, if you believe deeply that your collaborator's idea lessens the work, then be strong in your conviction, but do it without demeaning your collaborator. At some point, if there is a stalemate, someone has to concede. When you plead your case, do it with logic and diplomacy, and try to stop short of words that will destroy the relationship. Lauren and I are still collaborating and have reached a place where we can say, "That sucks," and move on or say, "That's great," and mean it.

Expect the dynamics to be different with different collaborators.

Some might like to dive right into the session, and others might prefer to talk for a while before getting into the creative slog. Some might like to talk for a long time, often about the inequities that songwriters face in the music business and how it was so much better for songwriters in days of yore.

This is true insofar as albums do not sell in the numbers that they once did, with a few exceptions. On many hit songs, there seem to be more writers. I counted ten on one of the songs on the Beyoncé album entitled *Beyoncé*, which was famously released as a surprise to great acclaim and with seventeen accompanying videos. That there are ten writers on a song is usually a product of many people building the music on a track and each receiving credit. This is a model that did not exist when I began writing but is now, in some genres of music, an accepted fact of collaboration. The results can be excellent, but the rewards as a songwriter, other than the possible glory, can be slim. I try to avoid those situations but would not rule them out. I have been involved in collaborations that started out with three writers and ended up with five, due to the artist wanting to change a few words and a music contributor being added by the record company without first asking the original writers.

In situations like these, you accede for the sake of a relationship with a collaborator or to build your credits. I call that "planting seeds," and it is about building a career. It does not necessarily feel good at the time, but because you were a team player, you then get the call for the next job (and the next and the next), and the pain will lessen. The seeds will have grown. Being able reach a point in your journey where you can continuously work at a job you love can make the rough road you had to travel seem, in retrospect, more like paying your dues than getting flayed.

I do not condone nor do I believe in the fairness of these situations, but I believe in being smart enough to navigate the politics of your chosen profession with your eye on the end game: a career doing what you love to do. Perhaps when you get into a position of power, where you can dictate the terms of your collaboration, you will recall the hurt you felt and not perpetuate the unfairness you experienced. Doing the right thing can also build great collaborations and relationships, and I have found that it feels good.

Lauren and I must always have lunch before we write. We do not dive into the session. It is genteel, civilized. We take our writing utensils to the lunch spot and throw out ideas, even, at times, writing them down. However, it is the mutual connection we establish that is the objective, because it allows for the uninhibited ebb and flow of ideas, which is the bedrock of a great collaboration.

Our method is about trust and, in many ways, love. It is also a fine way to procrastinate without guilt before getting down to business, because we need our nourishment to do our best work. This approach or attitude can apply to the way you live your life and easily to any profession.

I have always considered myself proactive in pursuing my career and being able to learn from my collaborators, as I did when writing a song for the Disney animated feature *102 Dal-matians*. I received an urgent call from Lauren asking me to come over to her house straight away to write a song for the film. Time was of the essence. No lunch. When I arrived, Lauren informed me that we had to write six songs to get this one cut, and we had to do it that day.

Fortunately, the great trust, respect, and communication that Lauren and I had established through years of collaborating eased the pressure. Thanks to our close and uninhibited collaborative relationship, we were confident that we could meet this demanding deadline. Establish collaboration, and you will be more productive.

The gauntlet had been thrown down. We blazed through the ideas, coming up with titles, lyrics, and melodies until there were six songs. It was a breathless, challenging, and educational affair that served me well when working with Hilary Duff, as I submitted close to twenty songs for each of the three albums I worked on and ended up with at least half a dozen cuts per album, including all the original songs on her Christmas album, one of which Metal Mike Saunders of the *Village Voice* wrote:

> *Speaking of Santa...an entire 10-song Christmas album from our girl Hilary...her first long-form effort—half of it very rocking, with one certified Spector-tribute genius track (written-produced by Charlie Midnight), "When the Snow Comes Down in Tinseltown." It's actually one of the best half-original rock-Xmas sets ever.*

JAMEY JOHNSON

From the *Boot*: "Jamey Johnson's New Music Is Finding 'My Way to You,'" by Vernell Hackett, May 20, 2010:

> *Jamey Johnson is being hailed as country music's new savior, with his cut-to-the-chase lyrics and those soulful, traditional country vocals. His critically acclaimed, multi-award-winning 2008 album,* That Lonesome Song, *left fans thirsty for more...And Jamey is now putting the finishing touches on the perfect thirst quencher, "Guitar Song I & II," which will release later this year.*
>
> *One of the album's many standout songs, "My Way to You," is an introspective look from a man who has taken many twists and turns in finding his way on his intended route. "It's about which way he went, and the repercussion from the next decision, until he gets darker and bleaker and is totally lost," Jamey explains. "He starts putting two and two together on the way out and comes to the conclusion that everything is for the purpose of God and it's all wrapped in the design of the yin and yang. That's what it is all about— you live your life for the purpose of God, that's the conclusion of it all. Yeah, you're gonna make a bad decision somewhere and they're gonna come back and haunt you.*
>
> *"That's OK, that's part of life, too. That's the message of this album."*

I wrote that song with Jamey two years before it was released as a single and almost three years before the album (which went on to win a Grammy in 2011 for Best Country Album) was released.

Jamey was in Los Angeles to do some writing and hang out in Orange County with his friend Jeremy Popoff of the band Lit. I was asked to write with Jamey by a mutual acquaintance with the caveat that he was an artist with no record deal but that he was a fine songwriter. I trusted the opinion of this mutual acquaintance, and because the quality of my cowriters is more important to me than whether they have a high profile, I happily agreed. Jamey had had success as a songwriter with a song sung by Trace Atkins called "Honky Tonk Badonkadonk," which Jamey told me that he had written with his two cowriters, Randy Houser and Dallas Davidson, while sitting in a bar watching a woman dancing. "Badonkadonk" is slang for a woman's shapely derriere. It was, in hindsight (no pun intended), a moment of inspired collaboration.

My wife, Susanna, and daughter, Shantie, were very taken with Jamey when he came to my house for our writing session: he was a slim, clean-cut ex-marine who was polite, had a Southern drawl, and was good looking, in their opinions. He has since let his inner outlaw emerge and no longer, except for the subjective description of "good looking," fits that physical description. This observation is only important insofar as it speaks to my belief in following your muse and letting your idiosyncrasies, your unique qualities, define you.

In any career that you choose, it is important to stand out, to separate yourself from the pack. In the field of music, this would seem to be obvious, but in reality, artists are often pushed into a direction that is supposed to be more commercial, thus sacrificing much of their uniqueness. In any field, be it business, academia, athletics, science, the culinary arts, show business, or whatever career you can imagine, there are certain defined

Leo Kaufman,
veteran of WWII

Bella Kaufman, aka
Bella the Barracuda.

Charlie Midnight, James Brown, Dan Hartman...holding lyrics that Charlie wrote out for Mr. Brown.

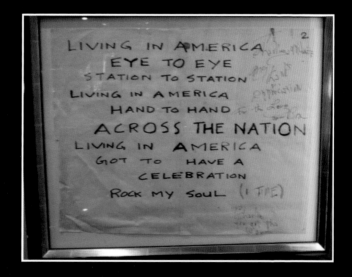

Chorus lyric Charlie wrote out for Mr. Brown on day of recording "Living in America," on which Mr. Brown wrote his respect and thanks to Charlie.

Charlie and Susanna Midnight at the Municipal Building in New York City on their wedding day.

Cover of the Charlie Midnight Band album, *Innocent Bystander*

Charlie Midnight at Max's Kansas
City, NYC, Feb. 1981, Pre-Album.

Susanna Midnight, Charlie Midnight,
Jamey Johnson, and Shantie Midnight.

Tyler Gordon (Engineer), Charlie Midnight
(Co-writer), Idina Menzel (Co-writer),
Walter Afanasieff (Co-writer, Producer).

Charlie Midnight & Syracuse University-L.A.
Extension students after lecture.

Charlie giving a lecture at the Clive Davis
Institute at New York University, New York, NY.

Charlie and Gola by the studio in Zurich.

parameters that you work within, some more flexible than others. But the great successes are recognized for their uniqueness. Jamey Johnson let his uniqueness come through in his music, and then it manifested itself in his persona.

As a collaborator, Jamey was a dream. Before his arrival at my home, I had listened to some of his songs and was impressed by them, as well as his voice. When he arrived, we sat in my living room and talked for a while, getting comfortable with each other, which, for me, is an essential element to a successful collaboration. Then I remember saying something like, "You're a great songwriter. What do you need me for?" to which he replied something like, "I love to collaborate, Mr. Midnight." I think that Jamey would agree, although I have not asked him, that being a good collaborator and loving to collaborate has been one of the keys to his success.

Although it was a bit disconcerting to be called Mr. Midnight, I took it as a sign of respect coming from his Southern upbringing. In Bensonhurst, Brooklyn, the legendary neighborhood from which I hail, calling someone Mr. or Mrs. is usually reserved for one's elders or friends' parents. My friends would never call my mother Bella. It was always Mrs. Kaufman. Nor did I address their parents by their first names. I recall my mother responding to being called Bella by taking the cigarette that was always dangling from her lower lip out of her mouth, pointing it at the offender, and saying, "Who are you calling Bella? I'll belt you one, you little worm." As I said earlier, they called her Bella the Barracuda behind her back. My mother would not have made a great collaborator.

I had some lyrics that I had been writing and a title, "My Way to You," and showed them to Jamey. These were the final lyrics:

Settin' fires and dark desires and nights that I just can't recall
I woke up flying with the angels
No one to catch me when I fall

I'm goin' down the wrong road, livin' by the wrong code
Chasin' after dreams that don't come true
Lookin' for the right signs, ridin' on the white lines
Just tryin' to find my way to you.

There's been high times, there's been hard times
And there's been times I couldn't tell
If I'm livin' a good life, or I'm livin' a bad life
I'm always livin' fast as hell.

I'm goin' down the wrong road, livin' by the wrong code
Chasin' after dreams that don't come true.
Lookin' for the right signs, ridin' on the white lines
Just tryin' to find my way to you.

From an Alabama porch to a dirty barroom floor
Burnin' bridges down I never even crossed
When I didn't have a care and I didn't have a prayer
I never once thought I was lost, somehow I knew
I'd find my way to you.

I had many of the lines already written, and Jamey related to them immediately and saw a spiritual sensibility to them that I had not seen. When beginning to write a lyric, I often do not concern myself with the meaning of what I write until it is written. If I am writing a lyric to existing music, I will absorb the emotion of the music and visualize a landscape, a setting for the story, and let the words flow. I let the sound of the words, and how they naturally meld with the music, guide me. It is a trancelike state. When I come out of it, I look at what I have written and see where I have gone and where I am going. If I like where I have landed, I will rake through the lyrics and rewrite and refine until I am satisfied with the shape and the feeling I have created. Sometimes the meaning of a lyric is obvious, and sometimes it might be open to interpretation. The latter is a certain type of lyric that I consider more mythical than literal. That was the tone of the lyrics I presented to Jamey, and he connected to it.

He had been through some struggles that he felt were captured by the song, and he contributed lyrics that made it even more personal to him. "Alabama porch...dirty barroom floor"— those lyrics came from the life Jamey had lived, which grounded the lyrics in a landscape that was more personal to him. It was a place that I would not have gone. That is the essence of a successful collaboration: it will take you to a place that you would not have gone, that you would not have created.

When I initially wrote this lyric, I had no idea where it would land or if it would ever get recorded. It was a meditation on the struggle in the seemingly never-ending search to find the place you were meant to be or even the person who you were meant to be with. It is how I felt as I pushed forward. I had a vision of where I was going and believed that I would get there if I kept on doing what I was doing—that I would "find my way."

It is satisfying to me that the lyric is open to interpretation but that it conveys the sense of the struggle. Jamey interpreted the "you" in the lyric as meaning "God." Someone else might interpret it as a love they once had or as a love that is out there waiting to be discovered. For me, it is not important how it is interpreted but that it has effectively resonated emotionally with the listener.

Hopefully, the result of a collaboration is perhaps not necessarily better (although it could be), but different in a wonderful way that expands your creative boundaries. In this case, I believe Jamey's contribution made the song better.

That was the year 2007. Jamey had no record deal, and I had no expectations about what would happen with the song. In 2009, I received this email from Jamey:

I was going to call you and surprise you today. We just shipped it to radio today and already we're getting played all over the place.

Thank you so much for such a powerful song.

The feeling of accomplishment I got from writing the song is the type of fuel I use to keep my fires burning, regardless of what happens next with a song. Naturally, I am always hopeful that the song will be released and even be a hit, but I have learned to take the middle ground between high and low expectations and relish the moment when the song is complete and I am happy with what my collaborator and I have created. When Jamey and I had finished writing the song and he sang it in that gravelly, warm baritone that felt like it rose up from a deep spiritual place, it was the epitome, for me, of a perfect, transcendent collaboration.

Every collaboration helps you grow.

BRIAN ENO

It is impossible to predict how you are going to get to your success. It is an unimaginable road you have to travel, but it is possible to learn something from the experiences of others who have taken that journey. In the end, the journey is different for everyone, and it is important to be fearless. Setting off into the unknown is scary, but it is exciting and necessary. While setting your sights on your ultimate goal and inexorably marching toward it is what you must do, it is useful to also consider the satisfactions you get moment to moment, day to day, on your journey and savor them. Each forward step you take is an achievement that gives you the nourishment and energy to go on to the next step.

Take sustenance from the new connection you have made; the creative collaboration you have successfully completed; the helpful relationship that you have formed; the great, exciting new idea; the growth of your creativity; and the undiminished joy you take in the doing. I relied and focused on all these positive thoughts and feelings to keep moving forward and to remain undeterred. It was a matter of necessity. Either recognize and be propelled by the positives, or disregard them and be crushed by the negatives. It is a choice that you can and should make if you want to succeed.

When Jamey and I got together, he was not exactly sure where the road he was on would lead him, but his passion and determination kept him moving onward, living for the song.

Three quotes from Ralph Waldo Emerson:

To be yourself in a world that is constantly trying to make you something else is the greatest accomplishment.

Finish each day and be done with it. You have done what you could. Some blunders and absurdities no doubt crept in; forget them as soon as you can.

Tomorrow is a new day. You shall begin it serenely and with too high a spirit to be encumbered with your old nonsense.

And a quote from Bella:

Go to bed with a clear head that you've done the best you can that day. Tomorrow will be a new day for you to go out and conquer the world, unless you don't wake up, and then your worries are over.

Respect is the key to successful collaborations in all fields. Being dismissive of an idea that is not yours is usually a good way to create a wall between you and your collaborator. Sometimes it is best to suck it up and try very hard to appreciate another idea, regardless of how great your idea may be. Sometimes only experience can give you the wisdom you need to navigate these situations. Sometimes you gain wisdom too late for it to be useful. Sometimes you might take some advice from someone who has had the experience and use it as a guideline in getting through those situations.

JOEL SOYFFER TO ANDRE RECKE TO HILARY DUFF TO JAY LANDERS

My association with Hilary Duff began when I met her manager, Andre Recke, through a longtime friend and partner in a recording studio, Joel Soyffer. Joel and I had been in bands together in Brooklyn before migrating, years apart, to Southern California. Joel and I had kept in touch after he moved out to California years before my own move. Soon after I arrived, we partnered in a recording studio we called Coney Island. Joel is an excellent engineer, and we worked together on many of my productions, including Hilary Duff, Joe Cocker, and the Doobie Brothers.

Joel introduced me to Andre Recke, who was executive producing the music for Hilary Duff together with Jay Landers, who was her A&R representative and senior vice president of A&R at Walt Disney Records. Each relationship was a catalyst for the next and evolved naturally while opening doors for further work and success. Of course, your coworkers have to believe in your abilities and your talent and that they can rely on you to deliver for them, their companies, or their clients the ideas, the products, or the *results* that they are looking for.

An ongoing working relationship can begin if you have not only created a comfortable and accommodating working environment but have also delivered the goods. The relationship will then lead to more opportunities. Delivering the goods and engendering a fertile creative environment is a formula for building ongoing collaborations, relationships, and opportunities.

After meeting Andre and hitting it off personally, he agreed to manage my career as a songwriter and producer and involved me in writing and producing songs for Hilary. This involvement led to my working relationship with Jay Landers, which evolved into our continuing friendship and creative collaboration.

RELATIONSHIPS BECOME COLLABORATIONS: JAY LANDERS

Jay has been the executive producer for the last twenty-three Barbra Streisand albums. My relationship with the storied A&R man, Jay Landers, began when I was asked to submit songs to write and produce for Hilary Duff. Hilary was, at the time, a four-teen-year-old Disney Channel star in the television series *Lizzie McGuire*. Jay was the senior vice president of A&R at Disney. This was a relationship that evolved into a songwriting collaboration.

As Jay moved on to A&R jobs at Columbia and then Universal, he continued to call on me to write for projects that he was spearheading. Jay, a lyricist, approached me to cowrite lyrics with him, and it was an easy fit. This relationship and collaboration has resulted in our songs being placed in films and with artists for their albums.

In 2013, we wrote specialty lyrics for Barbra Streisand's Back to Brooklyn concert at the Barclay Center in Brooklyn, New York, which became a PBS special available on DVD. Jay and I rewrote some of the lyrics to "As If We Never Said Goodbye" (Andrew Lloyd Webber/Don Black/Christopher Hampton) and "You're the Top" (Cole Porter) to reflect Barbra's Brooklyn heritage. This job gave me the once-in-a-lifetime opportunity to use the word "knish" in a song. As Bella would say, "Who knew?"

Without these relationships, I would not have been able to see my name listed as a cowriter with Cole Porter and Andrew Lloyd Webber.

Here is the track listing for the *Barbra Back to Brooklyn* DVD:

2. As If We Never Said Goodbye: Don Black/ Christopher Hampton/Jay Landers/Charlie Midnight /Andrew Lloyd Webber

Moreover, without my relationship with Jay and his relationship with Barbra, I would not have had the opportunity to cowrite with Jay and Bernie Herms (Italian lyrics by Marco Marinangeli) a duet called "I Still Can See Your Face" for Barbra Streisand and Andrea Bocelli. For her latest album, *Walls,* Barbra had the concept for a song called "The Rain Will Fall," which I wrote with Barbra, Jay Landers, and Jonas Myrin. Good relationships equal good possibilities.

Jay Landers and I collaborate as lyricists, and this dynamic has called for a mutual respect where there is little room for niceties. Our partnership has evolved to a place where we can say, "I don't like that; let's move on," and we move on. In effect, we are each other's editors, and that helps to expedite the process.

We are in this collaboration because of the differences we bring to it and believe that those differences create a unique Landers/Midnight product that is different and often better than we would create on our own. That is the essence and the raison d'être of any good collaboration in any field.

Separately, we have both written many lyrics for many songs, but we enjoy this combination and understand its value. We have respect for each other's talent. Jay has a strong sensibility that keeps a lyric on point as to its meaning, and this is a strong asset in writing specific types of lyrics for certain artists. His years in A&R have honed his intuition about the appropriate angle and subject matter for the artists we write for.

I have learned to trust that intuition, and it helps us to stay the course in coming up with a lyric that an artist feels he or she can sing with conviction. I have had many different collaborators, each of which has had his or her own idiosyncrasies and dynamics, but in all successful collaborations, there are two essential elements: trust and respect.

Because of the personal nature of writing lyrics with someone, being open to ideas far different than your own must be the crucible for your resolve to let other ideas into the mix. It is not always easy to let go of that great idea of yours. If you believe strongly that it is the best idea, then fight for it by explaining why in a way that does not disparage the other "best" idea. This is where it would be useful to be deliberate and diplomatic in your choice of words. At some point in the collaboration, each person in the room might think his or her idea is the best one.

There is no scientific method of resolving this if a dispute arises.

Sometimes you might have to accept the other best idea or be ready to settle the matter the way we used to do in Bensonhurst: throwing ineffective punches, grappling on the ground, and waiting for your opponent to say "uncle" while bystanders form a circle around the event, chanting encouragement to their favorites.

Use your words, and understand that we are all vulnerable in these collaborations, putting our hearts and egos on the front line. Right and wrong are matters of perspective. You can back people into a corner, where they feel threatened and want to lash out or shut down to protect themselves. Their ideas become surrogates for themselves and their self-worth. Coax them out of the corner by applauding their ideas while humbly suggesting your own. Or accept their ideas and move on, setting a more amenable atmosphere for the acceptance of one of your own ideas. As the late, great genius Marvin Gaye sang, "We're all sensitive people / With so much to give."

Here is a possible conversation between two astute and experienced collaborators:

Collaborator One: I love what you came up with, but I think that it might be too "on the money," and we need to think a little harder about how to say what we want to say without hitting the listener over the head. *(Acknowledge and praise. Mention the downside but minimize. Suggest another attempt, keeping main idea but revising.)*

Collaborator Two: That's a great point, but I think that we need to be very direct at this point in the song, and the ones you came up with are too oblique and, truthfully, I don't know what they mean, although they are excellent. *(Rebuttal: Acknowledge and praise. Logically explain why you want to keep an idea as is and why the other idea might not work.)*

Collaborator One: I get that, so perhaps we haven't yet arrived at the appropriate lyrics.

Collaborator Two: Perhaps you're right. Let's keep thinking. *(Concede that maybe both of you have not arrived at the appropriate destination. Keep traveling.)*

Hours pass, and all ideas have been rejected.

Collaborator One: Perhaps we should call it a day and revisit the lyric when next we meet.

Collaborator Two: Yes, but for now, let's put down a rough vocal, and when it comes to that line in the chorus, we can sing "Na na na na na na na" over the melody as a placeholder.

Collaborator One: Eureka—that's it!

Collaborator Two: That's what?

Collaborator One: The lyric. "Na na na na na na na." You've nailed it.

Collaborator Two: You're right. It works.

Collaborator One: That was an inspired moment.

Collaborator Two: I couldn't have done it without you.

Here are possible lines you can use:

"That's brilliant, and it could be exactly what we need, but let's keep going and see if we can top it. But that's brilliant."

"That's good. That's good. Let's keep that one in mind and throw out a few more ideas. But that's good. Really good." *(Breakthrough, but keep traveling. Compliment. Implied rejection. Compliment.)*

The concept of "best" is often subjective, and when there is more than one "best" idea in the room, how do you resolve that conundrum? The answer is that there is no absolute answer. It is a situation that calls for diplomacy, flexibility, and open mindedness. You are there to create a unique whole from two disparate entities: you and your collaborator.

The right and wrong of an idea is based on taste, intuition, experience, and possibly the wisdom of a crystal ball. Should you settle for an idea that you think is not quite right? Is it a battle worth fighting? In your opinion, does the idea ruin the song? Have your tact and charm failed to chip away at your collaborator's resolve? Is it possible that your collaborator's idea is the right one? Question the idea, but also question yourself, and you might decide to accede and move on. This will be seen as flexibility and good faith by your collaborator—good for the relationship and for creating a quid pro quo when one day the tables are turned.

It is also possible and often the case that none of the ideas are right. This is a subjective judgment that you might make but is not shared by your collaborator. You are faced with a conundrum: let it go, or stand your ground? If you believe that the idea will harm the work, then continue to compliment, reject, and compliment. It is worth the effort to not accept what you strongly believe is wrong.

Start your argument by trashing your own idea. Humility and self-deprecation are useful prologues to the argument that your collaborator's idea should be tabled and revisited after exhausting all others. This sidesteps a complete rejection. Be the diplomat who cajoles, making your point with coolheaded logic and a bit of flattery.

If your collaborator does not budge, then perhaps you should flip a coin. Whatever side the coin lands on, be at peace with the outcome, and move on. Ensuring the continuation of a fruitful collaboration might be the more important concern. It's your call.

COLLABORATIONS BECOME RELATIONSHIPS: DON MIGGS

In the fall of 2013, I went to Tampa, Florida, to produce a band called Miggs (Elm City Music/Capitol Records). I had been writing with the leader and singer of the band, Don Miggs, for over a year when I was asked to produce the band. Don and I had been writing songs together for over a year creating songs that the record company felt were good enough, and the company had developed a strong enough point of view to go forward with recording the band's next record. Don and I had also formed a strong relationship through hours of hanging out in the same creative plane. We trusted each other and were at the point where we could say, "That sucks," and move on without disturbing the peace.

Once you spend time with someone and the trust is there, "that sucks" becomes shorthand for "I know what we are capable of, and we can do better." Before that trust is established, "that sucks" can mean "you suck," which would be counterproductive to establishing respect and trust.

As I have said previously, before I collaborate with someone, I suggest that we meet somewhere in a casual setting for coffee or lunch to get to know one another. In Don's case, we first met at a house he and his family were renting for the summer in Los Angeles. Although I was not able to arrange a tête-à-tête before the writing session, we spent a long time talking and getting comfortable with each other before beginning to write.

The collaboration went smoothly. For me, the perfect writing session is approximately two-thirds schmoozing and one-third writing, especially at the beginning of a writing relationship.

I had no expectation of producing the Miggs album. Our songwriting collaboration was giving me great satisfaction. Because we had a relationship based on trust and the label gave a positive response to the song, Don asked me to join him in Tampa to produce the album.

The band had released previous albums with moderate success and had used various producers; one, I was told, had barely let them express their ideas. I made it a point before starting the album to lay out my philosophy that the band had to stand for something, that this was a collaboration, and that all their ideas would always be allowed into the room. Before we began recording, I told the band, "If you do not speak up, then do not complain after the fact." Once I gained their trust, I was able to chime in, sometimes with great fervor, when I felt it necessary. I rarely got any resistance, only mutual respect and trust.

We are blessed to be able to earn a living doing what we love to do, and it is something that should not be taken for granted.

Every project and every song is, for me, like starting over again with the need to apply the same attitudes and principles that help to make the work successful but also to make it satisfying and hopefully enjoyable. Some are less enjoyable than others, but each one that results in a work to be proud of is satisfying.

The relationship with Don Miggs, formed from our collaboration, got me the gig. Being able to have a successful and smooth collaboration with Don Miggs, Michael Lombardo, Walker Adams, and John Luzzi resulted in a product of which the band and I are proud. The success of any product is a result of many factors coming together, timing and luck included. I always have hope that the necessary factors connect and the projects I work on find a wide audience. However, I temper my expectations and take my satisfaction in the moment of a job well done. This is not only a realistic approach but also the way I survive emotionally to create another day with undiminished passion.

The Miggs sessions took place about seven years ago, and an EP was released in the US that didn't get much attention. Recently, I was contacted by Don Miggs, who informed me that the album, entitled Miggs, which would include all the songs I co-wrote and produced, was going to be released worldwide, by Universal Music, starting with Germany. No expectations but great satisfaction and a modicum of hope.

The same principles apply when collaborating with more than one person but with greater intensity: more patience, more diplomacy, and more open mindedness. It can be somewhat of a free-for-all, but you have to stay the course, breathe deeply, and be smart until the natural dynamics fall into place; be the diplomat and *help* them fall into place.

When I am working with a band of four or five talented and opinionated musicians, I have learned to let the ideas flow. It takes less time to try an idea in the recording or rehearsal studio than to argue about its merits. Doing so also creates an atmosphere of respect, conciliation, and cooperation, which leads to a successful collaboration.

Alone we can do so little; together
we can do so much.

HELEN KELLER

Chapter Four
RELATIONSHIPS

Without relationships, you will be treading water in the open ocean with sharks circling for the kill. You build relationships by delivering the goods: being a great collaborator, being a good friend, and being fun to hang out with, which should never be underestimated.

Sustaining relationships in your chosen field is essential. Mine have been crucial for providing me with emotional support through the down times, the up times, and the in-between times, and in continually providing me with job possibilities. Good relationships can be even more important in between the lows and the highs, when you can still see the worst days in your rearview mirror and the best ones seem to always be just around the bend. You feel you are doing okay but not making progress, and you are ready to settle for wherever you land. You are not necessarily settling for a lesser life if you choose to stop in a comfortable place short of your planned destination. You can find many satisfactions in the in-between. (But if you stop your momentum and find that the in-between is not satisfying, it might be a Herculean task to get back your momentum.)

In the down times, you are not in a comfortable place, and that discomfort motivates you to keep moving toward your destination—a place of imagined comfort. Your relationships will be essential to keep you going both emotionally and with job opportunities. In the high times, your relationships will be crucial for maintaining that momentum. The in-between times might present you with a difficult choice of whether to continue pursuing what you believe is your ultimate goal or to stop short in a comfortable place where you might wake up one day with the discomfort of feeling that you have settled for less. Knowing that you have good relationships to support you emotionally and open doors can help you make your choice, and if your choice is to remain in the comfort of the in-between, then perhaps you have landed in the right place.

I understand the weariness that can set in on an arduous and frustrating journey. There is no shame in choosing another path if the one you are on has become demoralizing and an occlusion to your motivation, blocking your ability to appreciate your journey and be optimistic about it. But good relationships, and the succor and opportunities they provide, will help you overcome your frustration, maintain your motivation, and feed your optimism.

IDINA MENZEL

When I was living in my hometown and beloved city of New York, thriving as a record producer, I hired an amazing singer, a student at NYU, as a backing vocalist and for some studio work.

I moved to California with my wife, Susanna, and one-year-old daughter, Shantie, and lost touch with this singer, who subsequently became a Broadway star, something I learned when a friend of mine called me and asked, "Do you know that Idina is starring on Broadway?"

"Idina Menzel?" I said, as if there was another Idina. I was not very surprised, because Idina's voice and presence were singular.

Years later, I learned that Idina, who had won a Tony for *Wicked*, had moved to L.A., and I submitted a song for her album, which she did not use. Some time after the album was released, I got a call from Idina, who I had not spoken to all those years. She said that she had always respected and admired my writing and asked if I would want to write some songs with her for a possible record; she said I was the only lyricist that she wanted to work with. I was touched.

We started collaborating on songs as well as a musical that we conceptualized and were in the process of developing with the esteemed songwriter and record producer Walter Afanasieff and the acclaimed stage director and playwright Tina Landau. If you are fortunate enough to see Idina in concert, she might be singing "God Save My Soul," one of the songs from our musical, and possibly another song we wrote with Walter for Idina's Christmas album called *December Prayer.*

Having good relationships is like planting trees that might bear fruit one day. The connection with Idina came as a surprise after many years of having no contact. It was a seed that I did not realize had been planted.

Idina and I began writing because she wanted to stay creative while sorting out her opportunities. At first, there was no particular agenda. We began writing a song called "Hurting

Kind," which grew out of her personal experience. Then we brought the bones of it to Walter and finished it with him. It was a satisfying collaboration that evolved into an idea that Idina had for a musical. We wrote songs around a thin story outline that Idina and I created and took the songs with our outline to New York City to run by Tina Landau. We wanted to get her interested in writing the book and directing the play.

We sat in my hotel room at the Gramercy Park Hotel, showed Tina the outline, and played her the songs on my laptop with two small speakers plugged into a USB port. She reacted enthusiastically and agreed to sign on to the project. This was the beginning, for me, of another intense creative endeavor with great collaborators of high achievement and respect. However, as I had learned to do after all my disappointments, I kept my expectations limited to the satisfaction of the creative process.

We went forward with think sessions between Idina, Walter, Tina, and me. We further sketched a story for Tina to further develop.

Walter, Idina, and I wrote more songs, and the atmosphere vibrated with excitement and even some great expectations. Then Idina was cast in a Disney animated feature called *Frozen*, in which she sang a song called "Let It Go," which became an international phenomenon and made Idina a global star and heroine to millions of young girls who knew every word to the song. Many have sung it themselves and put up their renditions on YouTube.

The forward motion of the musical was halted because Idina had to take advantage of the situation. I was excited and happy for her, and Idina reassured me that the standstill would be temporary. It was a surprise, but it also was not. The surprise was that, after being so enmeshed in the process, the progress came to an almost sudden halt. It was understandable but unexpected. It was not a surprise that things did not work out exactly as planned, and although I was disappointed, I had learned to move on quickly from my disappointments. And this disappointment was mitigated by Idina's reassurance that it would be a temporary standstill, and by the nature of our warm relationship, I was delighted about her new success. Today, years later, the musical has gone from being at a temporary standstill to being assigned a special place in our files of beautiful songs that are waiting to be heard. I do not regret the hours upon hours of conceptualizing, communicating, and the warm camaraderie that resulted in Idina singing classic Walter A. melodies and my lyrics.

Regardless of the outcome, these relationships were true and involved me in a flow of intense creativity that presented great possibilities. I have no regrets. Without these relationships, the possibilities would not have existed. The disappointment came only after countless hours of immense satisfaction that I would not let be erased by the disappointing outcome. There are no guarantees that you will get the outcome you expected. For me, each moment of creative fulfillment is a positive outcome, the fuel that propels me to the next one.

In whatever professional arena you choose to work, the onus is on you to deal with and get past the disappointments. Your relationships will help you to do that, but the ultimate responsibility for pushing past the difficulty is yours alone. Relationships are a support, a helping hand, and a necessary asset, but it is your passion, persistence, and ambition that will keep you driving relentlessly forward toward your success on this road, in this life, that you have chosen.

And I said to myself, this is the
business we've chosen.

HYMAN ROTH, *THE GODFATHER, PART II*

In the creative industries, relationships and career can be so intimately entwined that they become indivisible. When you create a relationship, it is often on common ground that could be helpful to you in your career. That might not be your intent, but that common ground could be the spark that ignites the start of a relationship that is beneficial to you, both personally and professionally.

You should not build relationships solely based on some false pretense, such as using someone to get ahead, but if there is an honest foundation between you on which to build a beneficial relationship, then why not? Certainly my relationships, all built honestly, have been an important part of keeping my career going strong. If you feel a connection is being made, then it is probable that the other person is feeling the same. Don't be afraid.

Having strong relationships is the cornerstone of having a lasting career. Perhaps it is the person you are sitting next to now, or your roommate, or a player in your current band, or an artist you are working with on spec who will remember you when his or her ship comes in. They will remember you if you impress them with your talent, sterling personality, and ability to hang out, like my great friend David Beal, whose story is, although I am only in it peripherally, instructive as to the importance of relationships in achieving success. It also speaks to having the insight and courage to walk through a door to opportunity when it opens.

DAVID BEAL

David Beal was a great drummer and world-champion hanger-outer. If you wanted some company, regardless of the time and place, you could count on David. He could hang out until the end, hold his liquor, and always be in a great, chatty mood. Being able to hang out with no agenda other than to enjoy someone's company came naturally to David. His openness, good cheer, and conversational acuity made you look forward to socializing with him. Bonds are created between people for the simple reason that they enjoy each other's company, and a relationship based upon a mutual appreciation, comfort, and enjoyment is never a waste of time: it is good for the heart, soul, and mind and enriches your life. It exists as an end in itself and needs no other purpose. But it can also benefit your career and open up doors. People are inclined to work with people they like to hang out with.

When he was in his early twenties, I hired him for the first Joe Cocker record I produced. We became great friends, and he became a part of Joe's band on tour and played on my second Joe Cocker record. David continued playing on tour with Joe.

On one tour, while Joe was opening for U2, David became friends with Chris Blackwell, the owner of Island Records, U2's label, and they did some hanging out. David impressed Chris with his deep knowledge of digital technology.

Chris had the idea of starting a film company to make digital films and asked David if he wanted to run the film company. David accepted and became the president of Palm Pictures. While on tour with Joe, opening for U2, David formed a relationship with the Edge, which led to him coproducing with the Edge the Grammy-nominated "Theme from *Mission: Impossible*."

David's tenure as president of Palm Pictures led to him becoming the president of National Geographic Entertainment. Today, his projects span several industries, including media and entertainment.

He has, sadly, given up drumming, but because of our close relationship, I have offered to hire him again if he ever gets the urge to drum or needs the money. Although David's relationships with Chris Blackwell and the Edge gave him opportunities that set him on a path to ongoing success, he will always have his relationship with me to fall back on if, of course, he takes his drum set out of storage and does some woodshedding. There are no free passes. Relationships can help you get the gig, but then you have to deliver.

NEIL GILLIS

A new publishing company, building for the future, had pursued me with very big numbers. They would also administrate my future copyrights as well as finance a joint venture with my new publishing entity.

It had been a sweet deal, but it never happened.

Four years of arduous negotiations for my song catalog had gone kaput. Four years of turning down other good offers, and then nothing. Perhaps I should have read the writing on the wall, since the owner of the company had kept reassuring me that the deal was going to happen while continually making excuses about why we had to wait a little longer. I accept responsibility. There is an old adage that says, "If something seems too good to be true, then it probably is." We human beings are very good at believing things we want to believe, and that is why "there is a sucker born every minute."

The man who owned the company, after promising his employees that they were going to have a home for years to come, had cashed out by selling to a larger company. We were all left stranded. The employees who were promised security were suddenly out of work, and in the four years, the value of my catalog had diminished due to it not being "worked." We were all screwed. However, I had made one great friendship and business relationship with the president of the company, Mr. Neil Gillis, who is currently the president of Round Hill Music.

This is from Round Hill Music's website:

Neil is the former Managing Director of Alfred Music Publishing.

Neil was previously President of S1 Songs America and also its predecessor, Dimensional Music Publishing. Previously, he was East Coast GM for Concord Music Group after spending 16 years with Warner/Chappell Music, most recently as SVP of Creative Music Solutions. He also spent 6 years as the Head of International for BMI.

Neil is a composer, classically trained French horn player and jazz guitarist. He serves on the boards of the BMI Foundation, the Johnny Mercer Foundation and the National Music Publishers Association.

Neil was out of a job that he believed had secured his future. I was out of a deal that I believed had secured mine. We commiserated with each other. It was less scary for me, because all I had lost was money I never really had; nothing had changed with my career, and I still had my catalog. My dream of buying a pied-à-terre in Greenwich Village so my wife and I could be close to my daughter while she went to NYU had evaporated, but my daughter was quite relieved. (The specter of her parents looming over her while she exercised her freedom on the coolest campus in the world had caused her some anxiety. She might have, while we were not around, let out a huge, earth-shaking roar of relief.)

By this point in my long journey, I was usually able to keep my expectations low. I would keep my focus on the work and not on the life-changing possibilities of a particular opportunity. So many of my opportunities had been life changing in a positive way, but so many had been nonstarters. Tempering my expectations was one of my survival methods.

This time, I had let my expectations soar. And I had crashed.

I had wanted this deal to happen so badly that I had ignored the signs I should have been paying serious attention to. There had been other deals I had passed up because the likely pay out on this one had been higher, based on predictions made by an accepted formula in which the earnings of your catalog over three years are averaged and then multiplied by a certain number. The offer I had received from this company had been far above that figure, with other perks thrown in. Other companies competing for my catalog had told me that if the offer was real, I should take it. Perhaps at the time the offer had been sincere. But as time passed—not months, not a year, but years—I should have sensed the hesitancy on the part of the company and that the deal was not going to happen. Instead, my mantra had been, "Why would they string me along when it would be simpler to tell me that the deal was off?"

I had wanted it badly, and so I had ignored my doubts and better judgment.

Maybe the company had intended to make the deal but other considerations kept arising that prevented it from happening. Sometimes there are no bad intentions and yet there are still bad, injurious outcomes. That outcome had fallen squarely on my shoulders. It had been my choice to pursue this life changer beyond the point of logic. Would it have made the quality of my life better? Would it have enabled me to write better songs, be loved more by my family, eat a more delicious piece of pizza, see a more beautiful sunrise, or live a more meaningful life? None of those reasons had figured into my pursuit of this deal. The lure, the obsession, had been the illogical amount of money that I had been offered.

Wanting the money had not been the mistake. Rather, wanting it to the extent that it blacked out my judgment and blocked the instincts I had honed through years of letdowns had been my big blunder. Your instincts, your gut feelings, combined with your logic make fine guidelines for your decisions. I had rationalized mine into oblivion. Mea culpa. Bella would have said, "What's the matter? You got crap for brains?"

My relationship with Neil grew stronger as we licked our wounds. We kept in touch, communicating constantly as we rebounded from what seemed, for a short time, like a fiasco but soon became just another disappointment from which we had to move on.

Disappointments can be the building blocks of determination or its wrecking ball. If you want a career, then choose the former. Each disappointment can and should strengthen your resolve to not be defeated. After all, in view of all the great satisfactions and the incessant pitfalls that I had experienced on my journey, this incident, for me, though hurtful, was not hard to get past. I took responsibility for believing in the imminence of the deal despite the warning signs. I had wanted badly to believe, and so I had rationalized the many questionable excuses that I had been given.

Take responsibility for your actions, and do not seek to blame other forces or people for a misfortune that might have been avoided if you had been more truthful with yourself and not ignored your gut feelings.

Your instincts are essential to your survival, and if you don't survive, then you can't succeed. It is empowering to take responsibility for a failure and understand that you can move past it and grow from the knowledge you have gained. Think of it as an educational experience about your business, your craft, your relationship, and yourself. You are stronger than you think you are, and surviving a major disappointment will help you believe in your inner strength.

Unlike me, who chose an artist's life in which the erratic and irrational ebb and flow of earnings is a constant reality, Neil, a superb jazz guitarist, had long left the musician's life for one in the corporate world, where there is the expectation of a paycheck on a regular basis. Now there was none. It felt like a betrayal, but one man's betrayal is another man's "good business." Still, if it feels like a betrayal, then it will affect you like one. It was an anxious time for Neil and his family. My admiration and respect for him grew as he refused to let this profound disappointment, this shocking turn of events, erode his humanity. Neil and I and everyone else connected with the company had had our expectations shattered.

With nothing to gain from each other but friendship and emotional support, my relationship with Neil was cemented.

The feeling of being betrayed can stop you in your tracks and impede your forward march toward your goal. It will happen somewhere along your journey and usually more than once. That is fact, not cynicism. There is no way to be completely prepared. Most creative people I know have a desire to trust the people with whom they are involved, both creatively and in business. Trust is an important element in being free with your creativity. You are exposing yourself to your collaborator, leaving yourself vulnerable. You are vulnerable when you choose to have your career guided by someone: an attorney, a manager, a business manager, or an A&R person.

I have, on occasions, experienced what had felt like betrayal, and each time I was taken aback, bent out of shape, but never broken. Instead, I get past the breach of faith by using it as a catalyst to pump up my determination to succeed. It also strengthens and reaffirms my resolve that, for me, there is no success without integrity.

I also might be categorized as a betrayer. When I fired my bass player from my album recording session, I am sure he felt betrayed. Technically, it was my right, but was it *right*? Together we had gone through the hard times, and then, when things were looking up, when it felt like the good times were within reach, I let him go. If I knew then what I know now about recording, I would not have let him go. Even though I rationalized my decision, telling myself that it was for the good of the music, I felt awful. He did not fight his dismissal but protested with great logic: we were a band, and while I had the legal right to replace him, was he not also part of the music and show that brought us to this point? Was it not an all-for-one-and-one-for-all situation?

The responsibility for this decision, which I have, for a long time, seen as a misdeed—as a betrayal—was mine. It did not matter that my producer, who insisted that it had to be done for the sake of the music, influenced me. I could have said no.

My self-regard immediately took a dive into the mud. My moral compass had malfunctioned.

Then the album and tour were unsuccessful. I had been weak and had put the dream of my stardom ahead of my better instincts. I had betrayed a friend and ally. This wrong I committed has stayed with me until this day, and although I will never right that wrong, my determination to never again be a betrayer has guided my decisions. I hope that the bass player might have taken some comfort in the fact that the album bombed.

After the band returned home from our fruitless tour, we were in limbo, not knowing whether the record company was going to pick up our option for another album. It did not look good, and eventually the record company let us go. That is when my karma caught up with me. I was unaware that a conversation was in progress among band members in which one of them wanted to find another lead singer. It seemed that someone was blaming me for the album's failure, that maybe I was the reason. The band had the right to go in another direction, but going behind my back was duplicitous.

However, the leader of the plot had miscalculated the band's loyalty to me. The guitarist, Phil Grande, came forth and revealed to me the tenor of these conversations and stood firm in his loyalty to me. I was grateful, and I carried on with the band.

The unhappy band member had not given me an inkling that he was unhappy with me fronting the band. If he had done so, then we might or might not have resolved the problem, but I would not have felt betrayed. Knowing that someone is unhappy with your work is hurtful, but nowhere as hurtful as being stabbed in the back.

Leading someone to believe that he or she is the only option when, in fact, they are not is a betrayal of trust. Withholding information and preventing someone from making an informed decision on something that affects his or her career and life is duplicitous. Neil believed that they were going forward, but the good faith had been one-sided—Neil's side.

Betrayal takes different forms but, when revealed, always looks the same—ugly. Do not let it stop you from trusting others. It may be the way some people play the game, but it is not the way the game should be played—not for the sake of success and not for the sake of your humanity. Being known as trustworthy will be an asset in building good collaborations and ongoing relationships.

It is more shameful to distrust our
friends than to be deceived by them.
CONFUCIUS

I have felt anger, frustration, bewilderment, stupidity, and the desire for revenge after feeling betrayed. But I never let those feelings linger long enough to let bitterness take hold. Get over it, and move on.

I was not surprised when Neil became president of Round Hill Music, another new music-publishing entity started by Josh Gruss, a partner in the private investment firm Gruss & Co. who is also a rock guitarist. It was Josh's good fortune to have

Neil available to spearhead his new venture, Neil's good fortune that Josh—dreaming as a rock guitarist will dream—wanted to immerse himself in the business of music, and my good fortune to have a relationship with Neil, who immediately made it a priority to forge a deal with me. Serendipity, in combination with relationships, manifests. Without recognizing and creating opportunity, there can be no success.

My relationship with Neil paid the dividend of friendship and emotional support, and it was fulfilling when he offered me a deal with Round Hill. Is there any doubt that relationships can be good for your career?

Don't depend on miracles.

BELLA KAUFMAN

Always recognize that human individuals are ends, and do not use them as means to your end.

IMMANUEL KANT

ANDREW CRAISSATI

I never calculate the rewards I might get from a collaboration except the reward of the human relationship. Nevertheless, within a business and career context, it is not untoward to expect that, somehow, the relationships you cultivate will be good for your career.

However, wondering how, when, and where they may benefit

you is a thankless expenditure of your energies. If you keep yourself in the minds of the people with whom you have relationships, then it has been my experience that when the project arises that fits your talent, those people will think of you. They will do so first because they like you and then because they know that you can deliver.

More than two decades ago, I had written a screenplay called *Boulevard and the Beast* about a haunted electric guitar that my cowriter, Jason Goodman, and I named the Beast. The protagonist we named Jimmy Schneider, an aging rocker who had been part of a marginally successful band and was desperate for rock-and-roll stardom. He meets a Bill Haley look-alike who offers him a famous guitar once owned by a seminal rock-and-roll guitarist.

The guitar turns out to be alive and jealous, and the Bill Haley look-alike turns out to be, of course, Lucifer. Jimmy has a young daughter who is almost killed in the climactic penultimate scene of the screenplay as Jimmy, who is now a mega star, is performing to a crowd of thousands, and the Beast goes wild, wreaking havoc on the scene. Jimmy and his daughter survive and believe that the Beast has been destroyed in its own flames.

In the final scene, we see that it is still alive as Bill Haley retrieves the guitar from somewhere in the stands of the now-empty stadium. Their evil lives on to tempt another musician on another day and to leave the door open for a sequel.

A young British investment banker named Andrew Craissati, who was working with a nascent film company, read the screenplay and brought it to the company. They optioned it, and after going through numerous rewrites, including one by a seasoned screenwriter who I never met, the film never got made. In the process of rewriting the script, the seasoned writer, possibly under the influence of the film company, changed the lead character's name to Jimmy White and the locale from Coney Island Avenue, Brooklyn, to Melrose Avenue, Los Angeles. That was my introduction to Hollywood, and glad I was to have an ongoing career in the music business, a similarly insane arena but one whose crazy landscape I was used to.

Andrew was blameless, and we remained friends. To my surprise, I subsequently received a phone call from him asking to borrow $5,000, which he would promptly repay. I was doing very well financially at the time and happily agreed to the loan. I did not hear from him again for twenty years and had forgotten about the loan. It is my belief that when you lend money to a friend, you should take your repayment in the good you have done and make sure that you have advanced money that you can afford to lose. It does feel good to be able to say, "Don't worry about it. Your friendship means more to me than the money."

I was living in the hills of Hollywood when I received the call from Andrew asking me if I remembered him; at first, I did not. My wife, Susanna, overhearing the conversation, jogged my memory as she whispered, "That's the tall English guy who you loaned $5,000 to." It all came back to me. I do not recall exactly the sequence of events that followed, but Andrew apologized and repaid me the money. He also filled me in on the course his career had taken the few decades that he had been CEO of both Virgin Asia and Universal Asia. Now he was embarking on a new venture in the music-publishing business and wanted me to be involved. I was moved by this display of unexpected gratitude and, having had no expectations of even having the loan repaid, felt very excited and amazed at the offer.

The venture did not work out, but an even more exciting one presented itself. Andrew had put together the financing to buy the Frank Sinatra catalog and asked me to also be part of that project. It too, crushingly, was not consummated, after Andrew had, in good faith, been in negotiations with the principals for over a year. That was the big one that got away as I was imagining all the various ways that we could rework the classic Frank Sinatra properties.

It was worse for Andrew, who had been reassured that the deal was his. At the final hour, the property was sold to another entity.

Andrew had repaid me the $5,000 and had tried to repay me even more with those projects. I appreciated his efforts and integrity, and to this day, we are great friends who will perhaps one day find a project on which to collaborate that will not fall through.

Regardless, I was presented with opportunities that would not have existed without this relationship.

Finally, business is a cobweb of
human relationships.

H. ROSS PEROT

Chapter Five
AMBITION

Ambition: a strong desire to do or to achieve something, typically requiring determination and hard work. The desire and determination to achieve success.

Do you have that fire, that strong, compelling desire for success?

Do you feel the urgency to carve a life for yourself doing what you were born to do—a successful life as you envisioned for yourself? Look around you. Everywhere you go, there are people filled with ambition; people who will answer yes to those questions. Is your answer yes? You've got to want it *badly*.

Ambition is not an evil force. It is not Gordon Gekko in *Wall Street*, a type of personality that combines ambition with a lust for power and money—a noxious combination that fosters betrayal and deceit, that extols as a virtue the insidious Machiavellian credo of "the end justifies the means."

I used to rehearse next door to a really cute, sexy girl named

Madonna in New York City, in a building on Thirty-Eighth Street and Eighth Avenue that we called the Music Building. She had great ambition. Everyone in the building was ambitious, but her ambition, in my opinion, stood out. In hindsight, we know that it worked out well for her. When she first started having hits, it was a bit surprising. One hit—okay. Two hits...sure. But then, hit after hit after hit, she became Madonna the icon. Without her ambition, would she have become *Madonna*?

Of course, ambition is not enough. There has to be some ability upon which to hang your ambition. In my own very unscientific opinion, Madonna's ambition was the catalyst that brought out her singular talent as a great performance artist. She creates events around herself, her music, and her life that transcend the pop idiom and ascend into art, and her ambition is her driving force. You can't become Madonna, Springsteen, Dylan, Adele, Katy Perry, Steve Jobs, Bill Gates, or Genghis Khan, or be successful in a field where the competition is overwhelming and flush with talent, if you do not have ambition.

Genghis Khan was arguably the most ambitious of all and successful to the extent that, in the thirteenth century, he amassed one of the largest contiguous empires in the world.

Ambition is simply, by definition, "the desire and determination to achieve success." It is neither good nor bad; it is whatever you do with it. So do good with it, and use it to achieve your success. I have thought about what might have stoked my intense ambition, and I think about my father, a factory worker who one day, while I was driving in the car with him, said to me that he regretted his life, that he felt like he had never tried to fulfill whatever potential he had.

I have quoted my mother a lot because she always had

some pithy, blunt words of wisdom at the tip of her tongue that, whether I knew it at the time she delivered them, influenced my way of thinking and acting. My father, Leo, taught more by example and influenced me by his stoicism and unwillingness to be broken when quitting a job he hated and having to take one for far less pay. He was unflinchingly honest and respected by his peers in the factories where he worked and in the union of which he was a staunch member since the start of his working days during the Great Depression, toiling in sweat shops and giving up his dream of going to college in order to contribute to his family's finances.

He did not talk to me about how I should be in this world. He showed me. There were no stories about what he did as an infantryman in Europe during World War II except that he learned to shave without a mirror and that there was no danger in eating food that had fallen on the ground. I learned from an uncle of mine that my father had been classified as a sharpshooter. But my father had never mentioned it.

Leo did not talk much, if at all, about his feelings, but the one time he did with great emotion was on a car ride from the Paper Box Makers Union on Union Square in New York City to my parents' home in Canarsie, Brooklyn.

My father, after being in the union for forty years, had been given a job as a union representative. It meant a better salary and pension when he retired. He was leaving a job as the factory foreman, working for a boss he got along with and who trusted and admired him.

He was happy with the work and the environment. Moving to the union job was simply about the money and the security it would provide for his retirement.

I was living in the city, and when I wanted to visit my parents, I would meet my father at the union offices and ride home with him in his car. As a union representative, he needed a car to go from shop to shop and no longer traveled the subway. On this particular ride, he seemed pensive and distracted. As we crawled in rush-hour traffic toward the Brooklyn Battery Tunnel, I tried to lighten his mood by talking about my day and how I was doing with my latest band. Instead, as we entered the tunnel, he calmly interrupted my attempt to buoy the atmosphere and said, "Charles, I think I've wasted my life." He went on to talk about all the aspirations, the dreams, that, as a young man, had formed how he saw his future, his life.

I tried to convince him that he had accomplished so much raising and providing for a family, being the best father and husband. He did not deny the satisfaction in that but said, "I did what was the right thing to do—I had no choice—but it was not what I wanted to do, not what I dreamed of doing. On the outside, I'm an old man about to retire, but on the inside, I'm still seventeen, with the same aspirations but with no time left to achieve them."

The more I tried to talk him out of this mood, the more distant he became, saying nothing for the rest of the ride. Soon, I stopped trying, and we sat in silence from where we were to Canarsie.

I did what was the right thing to do—I had
no choice—but it was not what I wanted
to do, not what I dreamed of doing.

LOUIS LEO KAUFMAN (1916–1993)

Leo had no choice but to do the right thing, because doing the right thing was part of his makeup. That quality defined him and made him an example to emulate. Still, those words of regret colored my decisions all along my journey. If you have the choice to pursue your dreams, then choose to do so. People all over the world, like Leo, do not have that choice. Choice is a luxury, a gift, not to be taken for granted.

The one quote my father gave me instilled in me the fear of not making the choice to follow my dream, of not living a life where I can wake up in the morning—or afternoon, if I have been in the studio until four o'clock in the morning—and look forward to going to work.

Ambition and motivation cannot exist without each other. You are motivated to be ambitious by events in your life, by people you admire, by a gene that you were born with, or by factors unknown that crawl into your psyche and push you onward toward some goal.

I can look back and pinpoint certain people and instances that might have motivated my ambition. I come from a family that, to my eye, was not populated by relatives with great ambition. However, I could be mistaken, because I do not know everyone's stories.

I do know that my father talked about having to leave school to help support the family during the Great Depression. He lived, by his own admission, with regret over not being able to continue his education. My father once told me a story about an uncle who joined the Alaska Gold Rush to make his fortune and, while there, was murdered for his gold. He had ambition to be rich and, I assume, was motivated by stories of the fortunes to be made in the Yukon. Perhaps he was simply an adventurer.

There is no compelling reason for me to credit my genetic makeup for my ambition, and so, in looking for an explanation for something that needs no explanation or cannot necessarily be explained, I defer to some traumatic experiences in my younger days to try to understand what fueled my ambition. The car ride with my father stands out as having kicked me in the head and heart and possibly forming my resolve to create a successful life doing what I love to do and, in the process, having the last laugh. But there are other grating memories that seem to have stirred my ambition to succeed.

I have found in my conversations with many ambitious people, some less successful than others in their careers, that often it is the naysayers and the moments of rejection and adversity that create this drive and ambition to succeed, if only, at first, to prove those antagonists wrong. While your passion for your work and the desire to create a career with that passion should, in a perfect world, be the only motivation you need, sometimes you need a little extra push to get you started.

Mrs. Weiss was my sixth-grade teacher at PS 186 in Bensonhurst, Brooklyn. The school is still there, and I have not been back since the day of my graduation. There was a system in which the classes were graded from one to six, with one being the smartest, two the second smartest, and so on in descending order. This system, in our more enlightened times, has been retired, or, even better, executed. I was in class 6-1, which, ostensibly and ridiculously, was deemed the class with the smartest kids. Each semester, the parents were called in for a conference with their children's teachers. When my mother went in for the conference, Mrs. Weiss told her that I would never amount to anything. Bella became angry and asked how she could make such a judgment about a child at such a young age. I was not there, but I assume that my mother used stronger language.

Mrs. Weiss did not back down. When my mother told me about Mrs. Weiss's statement, it did not motivate me to be a better student, but I think that it motivated my ambition to succeed. At that point in my life, I did not know yet what my passion was or at what I wanted to succeed. Once I had found my calling, I became motivated to succeed and fantasized about returning to PS 186 and laughing in Mrs. Weiss's face.

By the time I had my first success, Mrs. Weiss had died. She had been one of the motivators for my ambition, and I was robbed of my satisfaction of showing her she was wrong. But in truth, her perception of me at the time as a gross underachiever was correct.

Mr. Mullaney, my seventh-grade homeroom teacher, had the same perception of me. I discovered this not secondhand through my mother, but directly from Mr. Mullaney, who told me in front of the class that I was a waste. I do not remember exactly why he said that or my exact reaction, but I have never forgotten those words. "Charles, you are a waste." There seemed to be a consensus as to my unworthiness.

How did these two mentors of young people have such a dismal view of my future when I was not even thirteen years old? At that age, I was not talking of doing great things, and yet, for some reason, they had already decided that I would amount to nothing. Perhaps they saw great potential in me and were simply trying to throw down the gauntlet, daring me to accept the challenge to prove them wrong. Or perhaps they were insensitive jerks, hardened by years of dealing with children who did not pay attention in class, did not hand in their homework, had one-too-many unexcused absences, and seemed to have no ambition to excel—children like me.

Nevertheless, I was fond of Mr. Mullaney and did not take umbrage at his put-down of me in front of the class. From Mrs. Weiss, I felt hatred. From Mr. Mullaney, I felt concern. In homeroom, Mr. Mullaney often led discussions about ambitions. He was an advocate of following your dreams and waxed poetic about the subject of living up to one's potential; he believed that we have one life to live, and we should live it to the fullest. I respected that and often, in his class, felt inspired to dream or, more accurately, to daydream, which resulted in my thoughts drifting off in the middle of a lesson. Mr. Mullaney would ask me to comment on a discussion the class was having, and I would demur and say unashamedly, "I wasn't listening." It was not the first time I had responded thusly.

At some point, I had determined that it was easier to say, "I wasn't listening" than to pretend I was and give a ridiculous answer, or to stare guiltily at him as if I had been caught with my hand in the cookie jar. This type of repeated response might have justifiably prompted his "waste" comment.

I would have liked to have paid a visit to Mr. Mullaney after I had achieved some success to tell him that, in spite of what he might have thought of my shortcomings, I did appreciate his dose of idealism. When I found out that he had died, I felt sad. I wanted to tell him that I understood and that I had paid attention more than he knew.

Besides taking care of the hearth and home, my mother used to type addresses onto labels that would then be pressed onto envelopes, a job she took after my father quit his job because his boss was making him miserable. "Quit," she told him. "If you're unhappy, then quit." My father did so and took another job for less pay. He went from making $140 a week to making $90. My mother did not complain. She never complained. "It is what it is," she would say and take a long drag on her Kool menthol cigarette.

Bella, in her fearlessness and hardcore wisdom, had given me an article of faith: "If you're unhappy, then quit." My mother's sage advice became my rationale for quitting jobs and fired my ambition to work a job that I would never want to quit.

Bella was neither a dreamer nor a complainer: she was a pragmatist who had been through the Great Depression and poverty. She did not believe in being unhappy, and she was not. Nor was she happy. She simply *was*. You don't like your job—quit. You need money—work.

You want to dream of doing great things—do it. "Crap—or get off the pot," Bella would insist, which, to this day, I find to be a helpful principle for those wanting to succeed. Do it, or move on. Do not complain. Life is not a game played by a defined set of rules, played fairly, or played on a level playing field. Accept that fact. It is what it is.

There is no need to discover the roots of your ambition or for your ambition to be fueled by hurt and some kind of need for revenge or satisfaction that is never really satisfying. Your ambition can come from your realization, the keen perception, that the life you want to live, the job you want to wake up to every day, is yours for the taking if you are persistent in its pursuit, and that, without your ambition driving you onward, you will have to rely on luck. You can also win the Mega Millions Lottery at odds of 259 million to one.

Sometimes it is hard, when you are struggling and questioning your choices, to not look back and feel a bit of regret for not having gone in a different direction. Let your ambition stomp on that feeling, and get tough. This is the path you chose because you were compelled by your passion to follow it, and it will be your ambition that will keep you going. Passion and ambition combined can get you through the hardest times.

If you are fortunate to live in an environment where you can express your ambitions and imagine that you can achieve them, then do not take it for granted. When you are blessed to have opportunities and do not take them, it is an insult to those whose lives are devoid of opportunity. Geography, biology, culture, and misfortune can often dictate the limitations of life. Great ambition can possibly overcome those obstacles, and every path to success will have obstacles, but if by chance you were born in a country, a society, or a culture in which you have been given every chance to realize your ambitions, then perhaps you should not waste that stroke of good luck.

No one is entitled to success. We are only entitled to try for it. Your passion is the beginning of your reason to try for it. Add ambition to that passion, and you will persist. Ambition can trump fear.

For a few years, Dan Hartman and I had been having success as a writing team, and I was content to write lyrics, make a good living, and now and then receive a modicum of glory. After the gruesome fate of my album, and looking into what seemed to be the abyss, I felt like I was living the life of a country gentleman. I worked side by side with Dan when he produced James Brown and was in the studio when Stevie Ray Vaughn played guitar into the early morning hours on "Living in America." I stood near

James Brown as he was recording that vocal, going over with him the lyrics I had written down on a big sheet of paper, thinking, "If only the guys in the old neighborhood could see me now."

I had not kept in touch with anyone from my old neighborhood of Bensonhurst and had not been back to the neighborhood since the day my family moved away to Canarsie, a two-fare zone on the edge of Brooklyn. A "two-fare zone" is a neighborhood that is not close to any subway line, and so it is necessary to take a bus from the subway to that neighborhood. It seemed to me like a no-man's land, where many of the houses were built on swampland, and some had sunk so far into the ground that the roofs were eye level. The "old neighborhood" for me was Bensonhurst.

Perhaps if the guys in the old neighborhood could see me working with James Brown, they might have shrugged and thought, "It's a thrill to see James Brown singing, but who is that person in the studio with him?" Decades that felt like centuries had passed since my days in Bensonhurst, and memory is an unreliable source of history—my history with the guys in the old neighborhood. Still, I did have that desire—which I know stemmed from my childhood desire to be recognized—to be cool and, ultimately, to be remembered. That was the root of my ambition.

The question of where your ambition comes from is not as important as having it and then using it to propel you toward your goals. *How* you are remembered, *why* you are thought of as cool, and *for what* you are recognized should be your concerns.

How: As a person who has accomplished something positive in your chosen field.

Why: Because you have accomplished something positive in your chosen field.

For what: Accomplishing something positive in your chosen field.

But be ambitious while maintaining your principles.

I started singing in rock-and-roll bands because of images I aspired toward: Jim Morrison's poetic decadence and mystery; Otis Redding's transcendent, uncompromising soulful revelations; Bob Dylan's mythology and impenetrable persona; and the iconography of coolness. That aspiration fed my ambition to succeed as a lead singer in a rock band. When I fell short of that particular success, my ambition, from wherever it had germinated, had become part of my DNA. My ambition to live a life where my vocation and my avocation are one and the same drove me onward past what some might consider failure.

> *I have not failed. I've just found*
> *10,000 ways that won't work.*

THOMAS EDISON

I had never thought of becoming a record producer. I was satisfied being Dan Hartman's writing partner. It was a breeze compared to the grind of pursuing the rock-star dream, and it was rewarding creatively and monetarily. It was comfortable, but being willing to go outside your comfort zone, regardless of the fear, is an important factor in achieving success. Your ambition will propel you past your fear and allow you to seize the moment. Carpe diem.

Again, Dan Hartman led me into a new phase of my career. He was scheduled to produce a Dutch band called Time Bandits but had decided that the timing was not right and asked me to step in. He would act as the executive producer. I had never produced a recording session, nor did I have the desire to do so, and I was fearful of taking on the responsibility. Dan said, "You know what makes a good song. You've had your own bands. You know how to work with musicians. I'll be a phone call away. You can go to England and the Netherlands on someone else's dime and, if nothing else, see the sights in London and Amsterdam. You can't pass up this opportunity."

Opportunity stoked my ambition, and my ambition over-shadowed my fear. I went to the Netherlands, wrote songs with the leader of the band, visited a site in the north where the Vikings would party and vomit, enjoyed the many wonders of Amsterdam, recorded the album in the East End of London, and drove back nervously each night or early morning to my hotel near Marble Arch via a different mysterious route with an East End car service and drivers whose version of English left me befuddled and who were unfamiliar with the West End. Each of these journeys filled me with foreboding as I watched strange new streets go by through the often-rain-splattered windows of the cab.

Would this be the night of no return? Of course, I had arrived in London with some foreboding. When I walked into the studio on the first day, I felt some foreboding. When I was confronted with the technical side of the recording process, my foreboding became dread. I eventually broke out in hives due to all the tension that surrounded my foray into this discomfort zone, and particularly from not knowing what all the dials on the desk represented; the technical side of the studio was completely out of my ken.

The engineer asked, "What tape level do you like?"

"One minute," I said and excused myself to go to the loo, but instead went to the telephone in the office and made a collect call to Dan, who, although it was early morning in Westport, Connecticut, answered my call. I am sure that he must have, from across the Atlantic divide, sensed the depths of my anxiety and stupidity.

"Dan, what tape level do I like?"

"Tell him 'plus three.'"

"Do I need to explain?"

"No. Just sound like you know what you're talking about."

For those who, like me back then, are unfamiliar with the terminology, let me enlighten you. From *Soundcheck Magazine*:

"Tape Recorder Alignment by Curt Taipan

The terms related to 0 or +3 or +6 elevated record levels relate to the relative flux level (strength of magnetic flux recorded onto tape), not a change in the audio output level of the machine."

I followed Dan's advice and told the engineer "plus three," assuming he would adjust the tape level accordingly, although I would not have known if he had done otherwise. My fight or flight response was leaning toward flight, but my ambition overrode my fear, and I persisted, using my gut instincts and years of experience in bands to work out arrangements for the songs and faking it when anything technical came up. By the end of the sessions, I was somewhat familiar with the technical terminology and, to a degree, what it all meant. The door opened, and I walked through it. My ambition had pushed me out of my comfort zone and into a new phase of my career. An opportunity arose, and with much trepidation—but even more of a desire to seize the moment—I grabbed it, held on for dear life, and survived to produce another day. Another day came shortly thereafter with Joe Cocker's album, *Unchain My Heart.*

Dan Hartman had a willingness to hire musicians and singers and collaborate with songwriters like Charlie Midnight based on how he perceived their talent and not on their current success or reputation. Although Dan was not my mentor as a songwriter (we began our collaboration as equal partners with much of our talent already evolved), he was my guide as a producer and my way into production.

I had to walk through that door when it opened because it had opened, and my ambition did not let me turn back. Also, I felt ashes being flicked on my head and heard my mother saying, as was her wont to do when I was scared of something, "What are you afraid of? Whatsamatter, you got crap in your pants?"

Dan said that for him the timing was not right, and that is why I was given the opportunity. The truth was that he believed in my talents and saw a possibility for me that I had never imagined for myself. With his mentoring and constant calming of my fears, I got through the production; spent some quality time in a studio in the East End of London; experienced the savoriness of Indian cuisine in restaurants that did not ask if you wanted it mild, medium, or hot (hot was the only choice); and gained an education by jumping into the deep end, albeit with an Olympian lifeguard watching over me. I did break out in hives, but I consider them a badge of bravery and persistence.

Dan's generosity of spirit toward me as well as others inspired me, fueling my desire to mentor young artists and help them to hone and believe in their talents and themselves. To be a mentor is to pass on knowledge and hope for the simple good of it. For me, it has become a necessity and a way of honoring my mentor, Dan Hartman.

MICHAEL LANG

Michael Lang was the curly headed, leather-vested, motor-cycle-riding spiritual guide behind what was originally and laboriously entitled the Woodstock Music & Arts Fair: An Aquarian Exposition in White Lake, New York: Three Days of Peace & Music. He was also, in 1986, managing Joe Cocker.

As his venture into Woodstock would suggest, Michael is a visionary and risk taker. When Dan Hartman, who Michael had approached to produce Joe's next album, turned down the project due to a busy schedule, Dan suggested, again, that Charlie Midnight take the helm, with the reassurance that Dan would executive produce the project. In other words, Dan Hartman would oversee the inexperienced but amazingly talented Charlie Midnight—"amazingly talented" being Dan's words in his pitch to Michael. Not surprisingly, Michael, obviously feeling the good vibes and going with his adventurer's instincts, agreed—with a caveat, of course. I would be hired to work on six songs, and if that went well, I would get to produce the rest of the album.

My foreboding returned, exacerbated by the fact that this was Joe Cocker, who, not that many years earlier, I had opened for on my brilliantly unsuccessful tour and who had been, after I saw him perform with Mad Dogs and Englishmen, one of the main influences on my decision to be a performer. At least I would be on my home turf, New York City, with Dan close by. This was an offer I couldn't refuse, and refusing it never entered my thoughts. It did occur to me that my path to producing Joe

Cocker was incongruous, and I was not sure that I deserved this opportunity. But, truly, deserve's got nothing to do with it. Fortunately, Michael and Joe were pleased with the first six songs I produced.

Producing the next six songs felt comfortable, and the anxiety was gone, except for the normal anxiety that comes while working on any project where you have the responsibility of creating a great product. The studio had lost its inscrutability and become another outlet for creativity, collaboration, passion, and the possibility of success. My ambition—combined with a little help from my friend Dan Hartman—a risky move by Michael Lang, and a dollop of serendipity had launched me into another career, one that I had never anticipated or wanted.

The *Unchain My Heart* album was successful, and I went on to produce Joe's next album, *One Night of Sin*, which also did well, and which led to my productions with the Doobie Brothers. Ambition will out.

To have ambition is to aspire, and to aspire is to direct one's hopes and efforts toward achieving something. It seems to me that the striving, the aspiring to achieve something, is never fully satisfied, and that is what fuels our ambition. Get to one goal, and there is always another. The momentary satisfaction of reaching what you have strived for evaporates quickly and feeds your desire to get to the next destination, whatever or wherever it might be. For a moment, I was satisfied with where I was as Dan Hartman's writing partner, but the moment passed quickly when another goal presented itself.

Perhaps the desire to achieve something in those who succeed is insatiable. Perhaps it is about aspiring and there is no end game. Perhaps, like Goethe's Faust, the devil will be able to claim your soul once you are truly satisfied. It would follow, then, that whatever keeps the devil at bay must be a positive thing. Let your unquenchable ambition to achieve something good keep the devil away.

> *Great ambition is the passion of a great character. Those endowed with it may perform very good or very bad acts. All depends on the principles which direct them.*

NAPOLEON BONAPARTE

Chapter Six

PASSION

Passion keeps you realizing possibilities.

AARP

Passion is the fuel. How much do you love what you do? How much satisfaction do you get when you finish a song, produce a great track, perform a great vocal, rap a great rhyme, or create a great mix?

Always stay in touch with why you started down this path even before you had the idea that it could lead to a career. It felt good. It elated you. You had a bad day, but when you picked up that guitar and played that riff, nailed that lyric, or mastered that complicated beat, your day got better. You had a revelation: "This is what I was born to do; this is my passion." Don't lose touch with that feeling, regardless of the hardships you might encounter.

When I was living in what some might consider squalor on

Brighton First Place in Brooklyn, getting ready to go to rehearsal with one more band in one more roach-infested basement, I remember feeling a bit melancholy and thinking, "Is this going to be my life? Am I going to be one of those people who never 'make it'?" When rehearsal was over, we ascended from the basement and hung out on the street, and although we were exhausted from the five hours of repeatedly going over the set list, the guitarist started playing a Rolling Stones song, strumming his acoustic guitar. The drummer began beating on a wooden milk carton, the bass player sang a bass line, and I called out to a passing girl in a white vinyl mini-dress, "You can't always get what you want." She stopped and our eyes met. She shouted back, "Get a life, jerk."

As the sun came up and I walked back home, I said aloud to myself, "This is what I was born to do." However, I might have meant it more as a question to my thickheaded self, as in, "This is what I was born to do? You've got to be kidding." My memory can slant it either way, but regardless, "this is what I was born to do" has been my mantra, and that belief, thickheaded or not, has comforted me on days when I have felt dejected and nights when I have been rejected by a girl in a white vinyl dress.

Stay connected to that feeling, that passion. Don't let your idealism be tainted by the cynicism that your struggle and frustration can lead to and possibly poison your resolve. Hold onto your passion.

One motivating factor for why I need to work with and mentor young people is because I want to feel their unsullied idealism and passion. It is rejuvenating and a reminder that I am one of them, one of you; I am the same person I was back then with the same fire, and though the years will pass, the passion will last forever.

"Time is money, kid." A man with a big cigar who was paying for the recording session spit those encouraging words at me. It was my first time in front of a microphone in a studio, and I was in a recording booth in which I barely fit. The studio was in Brooklyn, but I cannot recall its name or the name of the cigar-chomping entrepreneur. I remember being so tense that I was finding it hard to sing in tune, and after being told with some accuracy but no sympathy that "time is money," my singing went from bad to disaster. My first session was a fiasco, but it was also the first test of my ability to accept failure and persevere. However, at this early point in my journey, I did not yet know that I was on a journey and that getting through this disaster would strengthen me. I simply felt that I had failed.

Sometimes it takes getting through failure to recognize that you want to succeed. You get crushed, but then something weird happens, and you get up the next day feeling undaunted and even more determined. It is the beginning of a realization that you want to do this, that this is all you want to do, and that this is the beginning of your journey. A setback can test your passion, which fuels your perseverance and allows you to go against all the logic that tells you that the odds are great that you will never succeed. The passion you have for whatever field you have chosen becomes the armor that protects you from the blows that keep coming. You have learned that you can survive, and you want to show that guy with the cigar that you've got what it takes, that your passion is so strong that you will persist until you succeed.

Without passion, the other elements could not be sustained. Ambition would peter out. Collaboration would be a hollow endeavor. Relationships would have no gravitas. Persistence would be a nonstarter.

Your passion creates you. It is why you begin your journey and what ignites your ambition to achieve something good. It is the energy that you emit that draws people to you and forges and perpetuates the strongest relationships. It is the common thread between the best collaborators and the most basic reason why you persist. How do you get to success without passion for whatever you are pursuing?

Even more pertinent, how do you continue to pursue your goal in the face of disappointment, hardship, and an indifferent universe without passion?

I have worked with artists who are considered icons, and the common element among them is their passion for what they do. Regardless of their personal idiosyncrasies, perceived wackiness, or calculated personas, my experience has been that, when immersed in the arena for which they gained their vaulted statuses, the passion takes over. Outer layers dissolve, and they can be seen plainly for what they are at their cores: passionate about what they do and intent on doing a great job.

JAMES BROWN, JOE COCKER, TOM JONES, AND NATALIE GELMAN

When I first met James Brown, he swept into a studio in New York City with an entourage and the aura of royalty. It was an aura that he had earned and had propagated in the halcyon days of James Brown and the Famous Flames, when his dynamic, stage-shattering performances stunned audiences and intimidated other performers.

At the finale of each performance, he would fall on his knees, and a purple cape would be thrown over his shoulders. He would rise with the cape flowing regally down his back and be slowly ushered toward the exit, stepping rhythmically in time to the pulse of "Baby Please Don't Go." Only, he didn't go. He would suddenly throw off the royal mantle and stagger back to the microphone while storms of sweat poured from his face like holy water anointing his coronation. He was: the King of Funk, Soul Brother Number One, Sex Machine, Mr. Dynamite, the Hardest Working Man in Show Business, Minister of the New Super Heavy Funk, Mr. Please Please Please Please Her, the Boss, and the Godfather of Soul.

What he was then is what he was in the studio the day I first worked with him. Walking in, he demanded the respect and deference he had earned. His entourage buzzed with the sound of privilege. But once he started singing "Living in America," the lineaments of royalty faded, and the passion took over his being. His talent was prodigious, but his passion was equally as remarkable, and the combination changed the landscape of modern music. What I witnessed that day was the man and the passion that created him. No frills—just chills.

Joe Cocker was never one for frills. Pure passion. Raw emotion. When I was in the studio with him, I was a fan, not a producer. Each vocal take was a performance, unselfconscious and true. There was no "punching in," a process that entails going to a section of the song and recording a piece of the vocal—punching it in. It could be a line, a word, or even a syllable. The final effect is one of a complete vocal take that appears as if the vocal was done in one fell swoop. It is a common practice that is even done with most singers, regardless of their abilities.

Technology has allowed us to do this for decades, and an artist who avails themselves of this process is not considered "lesser than."

With Joe Cocker, it was not possible to do this. Each vocal performance was unique. Joe would sing the song in its entirety a few times, and then I would "comp" the vocals. "Comping" a vocal would entail possibly choosing pieces of different performances and putting them together to create one complete performance. This was often, in Joe's case, simply a matter of taste and not a matter of better or worse.

When he sang a song and he was warmed up, it was always a complete performance. Above all else, Joe Cocker was a soul singer; the passion counted more than the vocal range, the pitch, or the tone.

There is a song written by Billy Preston called "You Are So Beautiful" that Joe sang, and it has become a classic. At the end of the song, Joe tries to sing the last note but fails to do so. He reaches for it, but all that you hear is the final word infused with the passion of the singer. It is the greatest note never sung. Your passion for what you do and how it manifests itself in your work will be the thing that defines you. Use your passion to define yourself. It will mold and maximize your talent and strengthen your resolve to succeed.

My passion for being a creative person has never waned. It has spurred me onward after what appeared to be failures but were simply projects that did not work out. When they did not work out, I was momentarily stymied, and it did not feel good; it often felt painful.

But then my passion for the "doing" took over, and I became

stronger through my understanding that I could transcend the pain by doing what I believed I was born to do—my passion.

That which does not kill us makes us stronger.

FRIEDRICH NIETZSCHE

Nietzsche's truism has become somewhat of a cliché, but there is no simpler way to express the sentiment. Your passion, if it is sincere, cannot be killed, and whatever rejection or disappointment you encounter is only an experience, not a final judgment on the worthiness of the path you have chosen. When you recover from that negative experience, you will have gained the knowledge that you are able to rebound, that your passion is intact, and that you have been strengthened.

An example of this can be found in the passion and resolve of Natalie Gelman, a singer and songwriter who I have been collaborating with for the past few years. As a teenager, she began busking on the streets and in the subways of New York City. The Staten Island Ferry was also one of her venues, a place where, because of the captive audience, she would do very well monetarily.

Natalie performs constantly, traveling alone in her car across the country with her guitar, amp, and passion. We speak about her frustrations, the inevitable "why that person and not me." The years of aiming for but not attaining what you think of as success can take their toll.

I admire Natalie because her passion, persistence, and ambition are unassailable. But she wants more—as she should, and as all who are on this indefinable and often-frustrating journey toward success should want, too. I admire Natalie, because when she suffers in the struggle to expand her audience and gain the recognition that both she and I believe she deserves, she soldiers on, letting her performing and writing lift her out of the darkness of her suffering into the light of her passion.

Again, deserve's got nothing to do with it, and the question "why them and not me?" is a hollow inquiry that can be answered only with the hubris of someone who supposes that they know what, in my opinion, is unknowable.

Natalie earns her living through performing and selling her music and merchandise. That constitutes success, especially in this era of "pay to play," in which performers are not guaranteed remuneration for their services but, instead, are expected to guarantee the venue a certain number of paid patrons. Only after that number is reached can the performer expect to get paid. It is an onerous arrangement for the artist, but a performer wants to perform, and the club owners take advantage of the desire. I understand the proprietor's need to make a profit in order to keep a venue open, but it seems to me that if someone works, he or she should be paid. If a performer cannot draw patrons to the venue, then it would follow that they would not be asked back.

Over thirty years ago, when I was playing clubs in New York City, making $200 for the night was considered a good payday. Split four ways, that came out to fifty dollars a person. We left the club smiling. And the money was guaranteed, a minimum amount that could increase if we drew a big crowd. Of course, we had to have someone watch the door, because the club owner might have a tendency to miscount the number of paid customers, and the miscount was never in our favor. Today, if a performer manages to get paid, the amount has not changed significantly, which is a puzzlement when you consider that wages have risen in all industries during those thirty years. In 1980, in the United States, the federal minimum wage was $3.10. Since July 24, 2009, it has been $7.25; more than double. But for performers in clubs? As Bella would say, they get "bubkes." But the landscape is what it is, and in the hardscrabble life of the performer, Natalie Gelman manages to earn a living—to be successful in waking up in the morning and going to a job she loves, mostly.

Sometimes it is difficult to love a job in which your ambitions are constantly frustrated. It is in those low moments that you must let your passion turn frustration into determination. Ages ago, after I was dropped from the label and before Dan Hartman rescued me from oblivion, I existed in a kind of limbo on Seventh Street between First and Second Avenues, going to various temp jobs. As a proofreader working the graveyard shift (midnight to eight o'clock in the morning) at white-shoe law firms, I was able to earn fifteen dollars per hour, which meant that I could pay my rent, buy some groceries, and go to the movies once in a while. It was welcome security after being unceremoniously discarded by the record company and wondering what I was going to do next.

The wondering lasted mere moments, and I soon put together another band and was rehearsing new material I had written. Once again, my passion for the creating, the singing, and the performing had gotten me through the disappointment. I persisted because of the passion I had and still have for this work I have chosen to do, which Natalie Gelman shares.

I believe that those of us whose passions have dictated our lives' journeys are all very similar. It becomes more apparent as the journey goes on and you encounter people as disparate as Natalie Gelman and Tom Jones; the latter I met at a home recording studio in Sherman Oaks, California. He came to record a song I had written with Jesse Harms and John Waite called "Chasing Down the Wind," a song which did not make it onto Tom's next album but which, no doubt, should have. He, as they say in the music business, "went in a different direction."

When Tom showed up at the door, it felt surreal. It did not feel surreal because it was Tom Jones but because it felt so casual—so ordinary—as if Tom Jones in the Valley at a home recording studio was par for the course, which perhaps it was. After all, Tom Jones had reinvented himself many times by thinking outside the box. His rendition of Prince's song "Kiss" was unexpected, and it sizzled.

You do not produce the vocals of artists like Tom Jones, Joe Cocker, and James Brown. You get the mix in the head-phones right, press the record button, sit back, and listen to an artist in control of his talent. As I watched Tom sing, I saw the same intensity and focus that I have seen in every artist, every person, regardless of his or her chosen field, whose desire is to be great—to succeed. His passion for singing was palpable. His vocals shook the walls of the studio with emotion and power, two words that probably describe any Tom Jones vocal.

I was impressed as Tom listened back to his takes and pro-duced his own performance, intent on getting it right. It is para-mount in your desire to be successful, like Tom Jones and Natalie Gelman, to be committed to doing the best job possible and having the courage to judge unflinchingly the job you are doing.

Getting to the pinnacle of your chosen field takes a combina-tion of many elements, luck being one of them. Staying there is a product of keeping the fires burning, of staying in touch with your passion—the reason why you began this intrepid journey.

BEAUTIFUL ANOMALY

"Haters" is a song I wrote with Hilary Duff, Haley Duff, and Marc Swersky. Hilary's manager, Andre Recke, had informed me that Hilary had an idea for a song and asked if I could get together with her to discuss it. We ate lunch at Mambo's Cuban Restaurant, close to where the studio was located, and Hilary told me about how some of her friends had started hating on her, possibly due to her enormous success as a Disney television star and now a hit recording artist. I started working with Hilary when she was fourteen years old and wrote all and produced some of the songs on her Christmas album, *Santa Claus Lane*. Writing songs had not been in Hilary's purview, but artists grow, and Hilary was being given the opportunity to express herself in the lyrics and emotions of a song.

I do not recall what we ate, but it might have been the excellent Ropa Viejo if it was being offered as a special, or my favorite dish, the eponymous Mambo's Chicken. However, I do recall that we sat outside, and Hilary described her predicament as I took notes. Many of the lyrics I wrote came from those notes. Hilary was excited about this chance to make a statement that could echo the situations of other young people who were beset by haters. There was passion and hurt in her words.

Hilary's very successful music career was an outgrowth of her immensely popular turn on television as Lizzie McGuire. I do not know if a career in music had ever been in her plans, but the opportunity presented itself, and perhaps as a "tween" Disney star, she had been ushered into recording as a way to monetize and take advantage of her popularity with her demographic. Why not?

Television is a powerful marketing tool for all products, including music. Ricky Nelson began as a teen idol singing on his parents' iconic television show, *Ozzie and Harriet.* His appearances produced big hit records. His talent and passion grew beyond the teen-idol phase, and he morphed into a fine singer and songwriter with his Stone Canyon Band. Miley Cyrus, who started out much like Hilary, has been determined to take the opportunity she has been given and has passionately seized the moment and made it her own. Only time can tell the historical impact that an artist has had on his or her culture, and even then, time can get it wrong. The point is that *why* you are given an opportunity is not as important as what you do with it.

It can be a revelation to someone who has not felt a passion for a particular discipline that when the atmosphere allows, they suddenly feel the passion. Perhaps it is a matter, for some, of being exposed to certain possibilities and being exhilarated or deeply satisfied by the doing. From these feelings, a passion can develop and even give you a reason for being. There is no rulebook that defines how or when or why you can and cannot become passionate about something, but when it happens, it can be the reason why you wake up in the morning and are driven to continue doing it. Or it can be a temporary force, an unexpected moment of opportunity, that gives you the chance to create something meaningful: a beautiful anomaly.

Chapter Seven
PERSISTENCE

It is self-explanatory: if you quit, you are out of the race. So, develop a thick skin, and find your satisfaction in the creative process—the doing. Hit a roadblock? Go around it. Fallen into a ditch? Get up. Don't expect it to be easy. Be prepared for the hurt, and let the creative process—the doing of your passion, the plying of your chosen trade—heal you. Let that be an end in and of itself.

The more you persist, the more opportunities will arise. They will come when you least expect them, but expect that they will come. It is partially blind faith and partially a belief in your abilities. The frustration that you experience can be disheartening and fill you with doubts. That is why you need to get back to what makes you feel good: the doing. I spent much of my youth and post youth pushing forward, questioning my motives, and testing my beliefs, stymied at times by self-doubt; but I persisted.

THE NEW YORK STATE WORLD'S FAIR PAVILION

From 1964–65, there was a World's Fair at Flushing Meadows in Queens, New York, and the 1970s space-age-looking New York State Pavilion was used as a concert theater for acts like Jimi Hendrix, the Grateful Dead, Janis Joplin, the Who, and many others. I was in a band at that time called Homejob. An entrepreneur named Howard Stein, who was promoting concerts in the pavilion, booked us as an opening act for the Paul Butterfield Blues Band after discovering us in our rehearsal hall on Coney Island Avenue in Brooklyn. It was a once-in-a-lifetime break that was sure to be our—my—ticket to rock-and-roll stardom. Instead, it brought me to reevaluating my commitment to following my passion, which, at that time, was singing and performing. Writing songs was not yet my priority, nor had I recognized it as a passion. However, I had started writing songs at the age of twelve and was the lyricist and melodist ("topliner" in today's jargon) for Homejob.

Being the lead singer of a band often dictated that you were the lyricist. So I did it.

The first song I ever wrote, many years before I began chasing my rock-and-roll dream, was a Johnny Mathis type of ballad. My cousin Jeff's girlfriend, Michelle, was a big Johnny Mathis fan, and they were going to a Johnny Mathis concert where the opening act was the Lovin' Spoonful, a band that I was into. I went into the concert expecting to love the Lovin' Spoonful and tolerate Johnny Mathis, but I left as a Mathis convert. I bought his *Greatest Hits* album and loved the smoothness of his voice and the classic melodies that graced the album. The first lyrics I ever remember writing were these:

Pretty little girl, with your smile aglow.

Sweet as the dew and bright as the morning sun.

Pretty little girl I want you to know I want
to be the one, the one to love you.

I was twelve and had no pretty little girl in mind, and I sang the melody in my impression of Johnny Mathis. I still think that I can do a pretty good impression, although it sometimes slips into my Nat King Cole.

Our performance at the pavilion was a disaster. Prior to that show, the band had performed nowhere other than at rehearsal. I was wearing a poncho and affecting my best Jim Morrison presence: moody and tragically poetic. The audience was there to see Paul Butterfield: blues, roots, and good vibes. It was a bad match, and the crowd, sitting shoulder to shoulder in this large open-air venue, was vocal in demanding that we get off the stage. We had two drummers, neither of whom paid much attention to what the other was playing. Our saxophonist had been given some mescaline by a member of the Paul Butterfield band and was tripping and playing the best solos of his life, whether or not the song called for them. Still, his playing was probably the best part of our set.

After playing some profound, drearily mid-tempo songs with important statements that had turned the audience against us, we turned to a song that we thought would capture the party atmosphere that the night demanded. The song was called "Your Mother Is a Groupie for a Honky-tonk Blues Band." (As I write this, I am thinking that the purpose of this confession might be to finally cleanse my soul of this transgression.)

For a short while, the song did buoy the mood, and the audience, probably fully stoned by that time, was bopping along with the music. Howard Stein, who had been standing at the side of the stage, appalled by our performance, now seemed relieved and, although not quite bopping, was moving to the beat. Then our guitarist broke his string and unceremoniously left the stage to get another one. He had not brought extra strings with him to the platform. Either he had forgotten or, in his inexperience, did not realize that a spare string was a necessity for all guitarists. The dressing room where the strings were waiting was a long walk from the stage. He was gone, but the band played on and on and on, awaiting his return.

An eternity passed. The song became eternal. I was frantically signaling the band to stop playing, waving my arms in unintelligible motions as the drummers banged away and the sax player reached new heights of psychedelic improvisation. My gesticulations went unheeded or misinterpreted. The guys were in their own grooves, jamming somewhere between fear and the freedom that is found in fighting a hopeless war. Howard Stein had stopped moving. I could feel his disgust deepening with each hit of the snare drum. Hostility toward the band was palpable.

"Be careful what you wish for, lest it come true" is an apt expression. The band stopped playing and I, the lead singer, had the obligation to confront the bloodthirsty mob that wanted Homejob dead. Whatever savoir faire I thought I had proved to be all in my mind and not at all in my words. "Sorry, but our guitarist broke his string and went to get another one, so we'll continue when he returns." My words were artless—honest, but totally not cool. I was jeered at, sneered at, and cursed. Amid the chaos, I thought clearly, "My rock career is over. I'll go back to school." We were ushered off the stage, did not get to finish our set, and never heard again from Howard Stein. However, he did pay us.

That gig could have broken my spirit, but after a few days of introspection and self-recrimination, I turned the negatives into positives by classifying this debacle as a learning experience. I resolved to never again be caught off guard by unexpected mishaps or unreceptive audiences. A passion that can be destroyed by one bad turn of events is probably not a passion that will stand the test of time and turbulence. In order to persevere, you must have that hunger to succeed that will trump the disappointments that you will encounter and drive your persistence. Look at Jay-Z, who couldn't get signed to any record labels. Vincent Van Gogh only sold one painting in his lifetime. Simon Cowell had a failed record company. Steven Spielberg was rejected from USC twice. All of them turned disappointment to their advantage.

I recently received an email from a close friend concerning the despair that a young man was in due to being rejected from a university's music workshop for high school students. He was a talented seventeen-year-old who had applied with the assumption that he would be accepted. My friend was deeply concerned about this young man.

Here is an excerpt from that email:

And then he got a rejection letter—he is now just devastated. He never wants to go to school or do anything. He had his heart set on going to this Saturday summer program. Is there anything else he can do? He is obsessed with music and has no desire to do anything else, but he feels like his life is over now that he doesn't have this part of his future.

My response:

I hope since this email that Jonathan has recovered a bit from his disappointment. One never knows why one is rejected. I am sure that it had nothing to do with his talent.

Choices have to be made, and if you assume that all the candidates were worthy, then some have to face disappointment. If Jonathan has the necessary passion for music and is determined to have a career in that area, nothing will stop him.

We all are constantly tested in our resolve to forge ahead after rejections and naysayers that have placed pitfalls in our paths. It took me many years to even earn a living in music, but I never gave up my dream. I believed in myself, wanted it badly and persisted.

Look at yourself as a beautiful example of someone who will continue to do what they were born to do regardless. For people like us, there is no other choice and that is the point. There is no other choice. What keeps us going is the creating. The creativity has to be an end in itself, the fuel that pushes us onward through all setbacks and frustrations and hard times.

Talent and desire are not enough. You have to have the grit and stomach for the fight. If this boy, or anyone pursuing any career that he or she has dreamed about, is ready to quit after one disappointment, then perhaps he should reconsider another route for his life.

The beautiful thing about art, as you and I know, is that you can keep creating regardless of whether or not you are at the time earning a living through your art.

You must be driven to create. It must be something that you
cannot live without, like your blood or the air you breathe.

Again, hopefully, by now he has bounced back and is more
determined, more ambitious than ever. At seventeen, he
has his whole life in front of him, and right now he should
be honing his skills, aspiring to be great at what he does.

Regards,
Charlie

It is common for the young to dream of having careers in areas of their interests. Sometimes it is because they have an apparent talent and a love for using that talent, and sometimes it is because they can envision themselves living the lifestyle of a certain type of career.

Sometimes there is a dream of fame, recognition, and riches. The thoughts I put forward are directed toward those who want to have a career doing something they love to do and for which they have a talent.

You can be talented in business, sales, art, athletics, academics, and so on, but the essential ingredients for success do not change if success means working at what you love. It might happen for you easily, but you cannot count on that. I do hope the young man who was going to give up his dream because he was not accepted into the workshop program examined his reasons for wanting a career in music. If he is driven to make music and to use an apparent talent that he was born with; if his passion for making music drives him to do so; and if he can envision no other life for himself than one in which his career is making music, then he will have survived this painful disappointment and persisted.

THE MAGIC HORN

Nine years ago, two of my collaborators, Jim Marr and Wendy Pigott, and I began writing a musical very loosely based on a dense dream play by August Strindberg called *Swan White*. I was, at the time, the president of the August Strindberg Society of Los Angeles, a title that gave me some good "cred" at cocktail parties and gala events. We had no idea how to write a musical, but we loved the idea of writing one.

So we wrote a few songs, cannibalized Strindberg's play, made it a bawdy farce, opened it with an S&M scene in a castle dungeon, and persevered until we had twenty-six songs and a book. Recently, we staged a reading at the Geffen Playhouse in Los Angeles that was quite successful in the sense that we got through it with a ton of laughs, a rousing reception to our songs, and without any technical failures. It was a major satisfaction for us to see it sung and read by a cast of wonderful actors after years of acting out the characters and singing all the songs ourselves.

We spent nine years, going on ten, learning a craft and creating a new possibility to widen the scope of our careers and our creative selves through perseverance, passion, collaboration, ambition, and our relationships. We fought constantly, laughed about it, laughed some more, fought some more, and reveled in the process—the doing—seeing the story and the songs take form and come to life. Little by little, day by day, and year by year, we persisted with respectful and colorful collaboration;

consistent and intense passion; constant ambition; and the heartfelt, strong relationship that we had formed over the years.

Of course, in any strong long-term relationship, you tend to form rituals that become positive—even spiritual—shared experiences that those in the relationship come to look forward to and anticipate, with the knowledge that this ritual is one immutable, soul-satisfying constant in an ever-changing world where the specter of an unknowable and possibly terrible tomorrow lurks in the shadows of the present. For us, the ritual was to schedule our sessions around noon and partake in meals of six-inch Subway sandwiches, sandwiches that we never ate outside of our sessions.

Sometimes I wonder if it was our love of that ritual, and, for me, the visceral pleasures of a Cold Cut Combo on six-inch honey-oat bread, more than the desire to write the musical that kept us persisting through all those years.

Regardless of why we persisted, we did, and now we have producers and are in the process of securing funding for a workshop with the ultimate goal of bringing our musical, now entitled *The Magic Horn*, to what is known in theater as a "first-class production." There are no guarantees, but we already have the indescribable, incalculable satisfaction of having gotten our creation to the next step and believing in the possibility that we will see our creation, one day, on Broadway.

I have been persistent to an extent where I've wondered if I was simply being stubborn and purposely blind to the odds against me. But maybe, like a skittish racehorse, you need to wear blinders when you're in a big-time race.

APE-LIKE ANTICS

My blinders were on, although I was not in a big-time race. The Charlie Midnight Band was playing a gig somewhere at another urban club. It is hard to recall a specific city. I kept no records, and I do not think that the itinerary exists anywhere, so it might have been Cleveland, although it also could have been San Antonio or anywhere on our increasingly circuitous and senseless trek of a tour. We would often be driving five or six hundred miles to the next gig in a van, trying to sleep sitting up while our one roadie, overworked and underpaid, drove ahead of us to the next destination in a U-Haul with our equipment. This was not the journey I had envisioned after getting my record deal.

In fact, the experience of getting a record deal and the ensuing journey being an inexorable ride down a dead-end street is common to most artists. Very few artists breathe the rarified air of stardom, where you ride in a custom-fitted bus with all the fancy accoutrements or fly in a private jet emblazoned with your logo, and have a rider for each show guaranteeing accommodations like a forty-five-foot trailer with triple slide outs and two entry doors or a dressing room filled with white flowers, white candies, and white couches.

I recall the show but not the city. The extreme failure of the performance was due to an icy wind that blew through an open door directly behind the stage onto my throat and froze my vocal cords. Sweating profusely, stomping around the stage, and working hard to pull in the audience, suddenly I brought up from my diaphragm a rush of air to sing a growling, rousing note, and nothing happened—no note, just the feeble sound of a choking word. Regardless, we had to finish the performance. Compensating for my vanished vocals, I jumped around the stage more vigorously than usual, forcing words out with a hollow intensity and counting the songs off at faster tempos in order to finish the set as quickly as possible and end my torture.

It would have been better for me if a sinkhole had opened up beneath the stage and swallowed me whole. At least then I could have received some sympathy and, if I had survived, talked with all my sympathizers about how great the show would have been had I not been swallowed by a sinkhole. But it was my misfortune to have been done in by an icy wind and not the preferred sinkhole.

Normally after a performance, the band would be visited by local representatives of the record company, regardless of the quality of the performance. That night, there were no visitors. No one came backstage to lie and say, "Great show, guys." I might have replied, "Thank you," and tried to make myself believe that my overwrought energy had saved the day, but as Ponyboy says in S. E. Hinton's *The Outsiders*, "I lie to myself all the time. But I never believe me."

The atmosphere in the dressing room was morose. I explained to the band what happened, and although I felt a profound responsibility for the fiasco, no one blamed me. It was simply a wicked twist of fate.

The next morning, we departed for another five-hundred-mile trip to wherever and stopped to get gas. After years of paying dues and persisting, and after too many disappointments to count and bouncing back, I had honed my ability to put a perceived failure behind me. I climbed into the van looking forward to the next gig. Then one of the band members began reading aloud from a local newspaper in which there was a review of our show. As he read the headline "Charlie Midnight and His

Ape-Like Antics," I sank a little lower into my seat, feeling like I was being swallowed by a sinkhole.

It was five hundred miles to the next gig. We went past towns, fields, houses, and telephone wires vibrating against vast skies filled with either sunshine or rain. Shadowy birds flew in formation above us, perhaps on their way to their next gig. I felt the same sense of comfort as I did in my days on Brighton Beach sitting on the lifeguard chair. That icy wind that, for a moment, had sabotaged me was nothing more than another test of my resolve and a reminder that I deserve nothing more than anyone else but nothing less either. True, you grow weary of being constantly tested, but if you want to succeed, what else can you do but let your passion carry you through the disappointments and persist?

Energy and persistence conquer all things.

BENJAMIN FRANKLIN

Nothing in this world can take the place
of persistence. Talent will not: nothing is
more common than unsuccessful men with
talent. Genius will not; unrewarded genius
is almost a proverb. Education will not:
the world is full of educated derelicts.
Persistence and determination
alone are omnipotent.

CALVIN COOLIDGE

Chapter Eight
SERENDIPITY

It was suggested to me that perhaps I could add an "S," denoting "serendipity," to CRAPP, making the acronym CRAPPS. The idea was a nonstarter. If I added the "S," to make it CRAPPS, it would sound like "craps," a gambling game played with dice. It would then appear that I was comparing your chance of achieving success to a roll of the dice which would betray the point of this book. Or, if you didn't read the subtitle, then it might be perceived as a book about...playing the game of craps. So, I quickly moved past that idea.

Serendipitous events occur that can feel like miracles, as if they come from some inexplicable, unknowable force to grace your journey. But the miracle will usually be the result of accountable, quantifiable circumstances: the result of your dedication to that journey; your commitment to producing excellent work; and the culmination of the collaboration, relationships, ambition, passion and persistence that I have limned in the previous chapters.

JONI MITCHELL

"How did you get Joni Mitchell to cover 'How Do You Stop'?"

I have had that question posed to me a few times, and the answer I always give is, "Serendipity—the occurrence and development of events by chance in a happy or beneficial way." There is no logic behind these types of events, but in the case of Ms. Mitchell covering my song, it would not have happened if the song had not been out in the world. I have learned that if you don't put something out there, then you are relying only on serendipity.

This reminds me of a friend of mine back in my Brooklyn scuffling days who was a particularly handsome guy, often stoned and without much apparent ambition. At the time, we were working together as messengers for the same law firm on Wall Street, which is an honorable line of work, but he seemed to have no other plans. I assumed either he was satisfied in that position or it was a way to earn a living while he dreamed of doing something different.

We were sitting in my apartment on Flatbush Avenue near Avenue J, and I was talking about my working toward having a successful band, creating music that would affect people the way Hendrix, Otis Redding, Janis Joplin, and Bob Dylan, among others, had affected me. I was rehearsing my latest band five days a week, four hours a night, after working during the day. My friend also had dreams. He said, "I'm gonna make it, too."

"How?" I asked.

"My looks," he answered. "I'm gonna be discovered walking down the street."

"On Flatbush Avenue?" I asked.

"Yeah," he answered.

I was a little upset that he said he was going make it because of his good looks, as if it was equivalent to my working hard to succeed through my music, and I told him so. "Hey man," he said, "you never know, do you?" Then he took another toke and nodded his head as if he was imagining his future stardom. He was right. You never know. Deserve's got nothing to do with it. However, I have a belief based on nothing but instinct that serendipity does not happen to those who are counting on it for their success, especially if they are counting on it to find them on Flatbush Avenue near Avenue J.

It was amazing happenstance that led to Joni Mitchell recording "How Do You Stop." Serendipity, again, was at work. Dan Hartman, who, by chance, ran into Joni Mitchell while he was visiting Los Angeles, told the story to me. He introduced himself as a big fan of Ms. Mitchell, and she recognized his name. She had been watching the Cinemax special *James Brown and Friends* and was taken with Mr. Brown's rendition of "How Do You Stop," which he had recorded on his *Gravity* album. Dan had produced the album, he and I had written all the songs, and we had been there in Detroit at the filming of the special, joining Mr. Brown, Aretha Franklin, Wilson Pickett, Joe Cocker, Robert Palmer, Billy Vera, and the JBs onstage for the grand finale rendition of "Living in America."

It seems that Joni Mitchell had watched the special and then learned to play "How Do You Stop," albeit with her own chord inversions, a melody that she adjusted to her own inimitable vocal style, and with one small lyric change, which I loved. Dan and I had no knowledge that this had occurred or, as Dan was told, that Ms. Mitchell had been performing the song. Then she recorded it on her *Turbulent Indigo* album and released it as a single. The album won a Grammy.

"How did you get Joni Mitchell to cover 'How Do You Stop'?"

First, Dan Hartman and I had to write it, and James Brown had to record it and then perform it on a television show that was seen by Joni Mitchell, who liked it enough to learn it, change it to fit her style, perform it, and then record it. Serendipity for sure, but we allowed there to be an opportunity for serendipity by writing the song, creating something, and putting it out there. If you don't put it out there, then, to paraphrase Gertrude Stein, "There will be no there there." And no "there," no serendipity.

THE BODYGUARD

I had written a song with Marc Swersky and Francesca Beghe called "Trust in Me," which Joe recorded on his *Unchain My Heart* album, which I produced. It is a duet with the singular Australian soul singer, Renee Geyer. Kevin Costner was a Joe Cocker aficionado and was starring in and coproducing a film called *The Bodyguard*. His costar was the legendary Whitney Houston. The story (as told to me by Pat Lucas, who was, at the time, the executive vice president of the EMI Music Publishing Film Division) was that "Trust in Me" was being used as a temp track in post-production of the film, and instead of replacing it in the final cut, as was normal procedure, Mr. Costner, the Joe Cocker fan, suggested keeping it in, which they did. As a result, I had produced and cowritten a song on an album that went on to win a Grammy and, more deliciously, sold over forty million albums.

Renee Geyer, however, was replaced on the song with the

higher-profile artist Sass Jordan. Ms. Jordan was an excellent artist, but Ms. Geyer was a powerhouse, matching Joe Cocker note for note in intensity and soul. I understood the reasoning and that, in the final analysis, the music business is a business first—and second and even third—and that art and commerce exist uneasily side by side, using each other for their own purposes that converge, conflict, and often end up at war with each other. Commerce and its commanders may win many victories, but art will win the war. History will remember the art and the artist, with little notice given to the business entity or the generals in charge. Ultimate victor—art.

Mr. Costner had previously used a song in the film *Bull Durham*, sung by Joe Cocker, called "A Woman Loves a Man," which I had cowritten with Dan Hartman. It was also on the *Unchain My Heart* album that I produced. Obviously, Kevin Costner had been listening to that album, and his love of Joe Cocker and, I assume, the *Unchain My Heart* album, had inured serendipitously to my benefit. The song went on to be nominated for a Golden Globe. Both the film and the soundtrack album were successes. To date, I have never met Kevin Costner and been able to thank him, but I have never stopped appreciating his positive affect on my career as well as lauding, to whoever was interested in listening, his excellent taste in music.

In the final scene of *Bull Durham*, Kevin Costner and Susan Sarandon dance together to the lilting and romantic strains of "A Woman Loves a Man," a song I had not pitched for the film. I sat in the movie theater with my family, viewing the film for the first time, waiting as the credits rolled to see my name and Dan Hartman's listed so that we could all revel in a brief moment of glory and satisfaction. The song credits are the last ones to roll, and often the theater is empty by the time they do. So we waited. Finally, when our credits appeared on the screen, they appeared as "When a Man Loves a Woman," written by Calvin Lewis and Andrew Wright.

Although we were nominated for a Golden Globe for the song, even the Golden Globe site has the nomination for the song and writers listed incorrectly. I have tried, to no avail, through the years to have them correct the mistake. As you can imagine, I was somewhat angry at first, and I had no recourse. The film company was not going to take back all the reels of film and then reprint the closing credits. Once again, deserve had nothing to do with it.

Serendipity has been very good to me. Much of the good with which I have been blessed has been due to a happy series of circumstances that I am grateful for but which would not have happened if I had not put the work out there. In the scheme of the unknowable universe, perhaps there is a tradeoff of some kind that creates a balance. Put it out there, and give serendipity a chance.

Happiness can only exist in acceptance.

GEORGE ORWELL

Chapter Nine

SOME THOUGHTS ABOUT SONGWRITING

AN APOLOGIA FOR THIS BOOK NOT BEING ABOUT SONGWRITING

Unloading trains was work. Checking groceries at Waldbaum's was work. My father cutting cardboard boxes in a factory was work. Although I work hard at songwriting, it never feels like work.

This book is not a primer on songwriting or how to forge a career as a songwriter. It is not my life as a road map to becoming a successful songwriter. If I were successful at any other job, my anecdotes would have detailed how I used CRAPP to achieve success at that job.

However, because there might be a few songwriters who feel cheated because they bought this book expecting to get a few insights into the process of songwriting from a successful songwriter, I am including this chapter.

There is no ABC of songwriting, no empirical formula that is guaranteed to work. Be inspired. Work hard. Write, write, write. Learn from listening, collaborating, and doing. Let your idiosyncrasies loose. Write a fifteen-minute song if you feel inspired, but never forget that you are working in a popular medium, and one of your desires is to be a communicator. We all want to write songs that affect an audience.

Very few songs affect every audience. There are billions of people in the world. If a song sells ten million copies, then most people in the world have not bought it.

There are amazing music artists all over the world, most of whom we have never heard. You want to be heard, and we are privileged to live in an environment that allows for that possibility. It is not our birthright to have an audience, but it is our good fortune to have that possibility. So perhaps it is incumbent upon us to not waste the opportunity.

Is it important to be well read to be a good lyricist? This was a question I was recently asked in a radio interview. Of course, you need some vocabulary in order to express yourself with a twist of freshness and, now and then, be able to throw in an unexpected word or two. When I heard the song "Titanium," by Sia, I liked the use of that word. It felt fresh. Without knowing the rest of the lyrics, I immediately reacted. The chorus made an impression on me. Sometimes that is all you need in a pop song—one cool word that sticks out.

For a lyricist who wants to have as broad a range as possible, it could be useful to have access to a wider range of words in order to express your thoughts in more interesting ways. Words are the tools of the writer's trade, and it is an advantage to have the right tools handy in order to do the best job.

Reading can broaden your point of view, highlight things you would not have otherwise thought of, and give you access to words that you might not have otherwise used. It can be useful to be a reader and have a wide vocabulary, but it is not necessary. I think, for me, it has helped form some of the philosophical underpinnings of my lyrics, but simply living and surviving can do that. But really, who knows?

A lyric is only one part of a song. The music, the arrangement, and the vocals all help to create the desired effect. A great melody can carry a mundane lyric. A great vocal on top of that can carry it even further. It is a mysterious combination of elements that can create a memorable recording. And a memorable recording is not necessarily the same thing as a great song. "You Really Got Me," the classic Kinks song, is a simple lyric that I think is great. But would it be great without the music?

I can't teach someone to write a song, but maybe, in many cases, I can suggest how to make a song better if I believe that the song has not reached its potential. My songwriting developed from listening to a transistor radio and going to sleep with it under my pillow.

Learning how to write a song is about doing and listening and doing some more and listening some more. Every great songwriter has been influenced by what he or she listens to, and then that influence is filtered through his or her own vision and idiosyncrasies. Have the guts to go with your own muse but the open mindedness to allow other ideas into the mix.

James Brown, Barbra Streisand, Joni Mitchell, Billy Joel, Cher, Hilary Duff, Christina Aguilera, Chaka Khan, Spunkadelic of the song "9.95" from Teenage Mutant Ninja Turtles, Big Time Rush, Joe Cocker, Miranda Cosgrove, and Jamey Johnson—each one called for a different point of view, but my job didn't change. Understand the context, and write a song that fits the artist.

I was asked in an interview how I could write for such a range of artists. The answer was: survival. I developed the ability to move through different genres, empathize with an artist's point of view, and then write something to fit that vision.

I do not make a judgment about the artist when I take an assignment. I respect the job and the artist. What matters is the song. I got as much satisfaction from cowriting "So Yesterday" for Hilary Duff as I did from writing "Living in America" for James Brown.

Why? Because I live for the moment when the song is written and it is everything I hoped it would be. When that moment occurs, I am satiated. I feel the same each time I reach that point, and, to steal a line from James Brown, "I feel good!"

After all, the Hilary Duff albums that I had numerous songs on sold millions of copies. Although "Living in America" was a worldwide hit and has become a classic, the album sales did not go into the millions. Satisfaction comes in many forms.

I must admit, however, that there was some special satisfaction after the fact in having written a single that was sung by Joni Mitchell, one of the great and influential artists in music, and of having her sing my lyrics in a duet with Seal. And I do remember working with James Brown, being in the studio recording the vocal for "Living in America," going over the lyrics with him, and thinking, "If only the kids in my old neighborhood could see me now."

I can't teach you how to write a song. The only formula that I adhere to is "don't bore the listener." I like to write hooks: choruses that are memorable. That doesn't mean that you have to write that kind of hook, but you should have some kind of hook: a guitar riff, a drum pattern, a new sound—any of these elements can be and have been hooks in hit songs.

A three-to-four-minute time for a pop song is the generally accepted standard, but it used to be a minute and a half. There is a great song called "Ain't No Sunshine"—a classic. It is ninety seconds long. In my opinion, it's a perfect song—minimalist, you might say. How do you create a formula from that? It is a convergence of beautiful elements: melody, lyric, and performance. Would it have been a hit song without any of these elements? What do you think?

There is a song called "Time Has Come Today," by a group called the Chambers Brothers. The album version is over eleven minutes long, an opus, and was a classic in its time. Of course, enjoying it had a lot to do with being stoned when you listened, but still—do you think it would have been a classic without the legions of '60s-era stoners and trippers who were grooving in a psychedelic haze?

SO WHAT ARE THE RULES?

What do you think makes a hit song? What do you think makes a great song? Are they necessarily one and the same? If a song is a hit, does that make it a great song? Can there ever be a standardized measurement of what makes a song great, or a hit, or a terrible song? Are any of these questions answerable? The only reason to ask these questions is perhaps to deduce that there are many answers, and there are none.

While you are spending your time trying to come up with an answer in the hope of finding the key to writing a great song or a hit song, someone else is spending his or her time writing and rewriting and rewriting, because all writing is rewriting (to paraphrase Hemingway). Dig in, start the process, and be hard on yourself. Use your instincts. Don't accept an idea that doesn't feel right. Reach down deep for the one that *does* feel right. Your instinct is all that you have as an artist. By doing and doing and doing, you will hone that instinct and, one day, hopefully, write a great song—even a hit song.

When you are a successful songwriter, you might be able to quantify your own personal, idiosyncratic formula, the one that, by doing and doing, you have found to be successful *for you*. Does that mean that if someone else copies that formula they too will be successful?

Develop your own formula. Be inspired. Learn from listening to and being inspired by the writers you admire and the songs you love. Let them sink into your conscious mind and merge with your subconscious. Learn from your collaborators. Let them learn from you. Do it. Do it. Do it. Be inspired. The moment will come when you will not have to strive to be unique—you *will* be unique. Your songs will have whispers of those that have influenced you. You will have found your own voice by doing, doing, doing.

I never wanted to be a songwriter. I wanted to be a rock-and-roll star, a lead singer in a famous band. I wrote songs for myself as an artist. Is that different from writing songs for other artists? What do you think? If it is different, then how is it different? How is it the same?

After the *Charlie Midnight* album debacle, I was blessed to become the writing partner of Dan Hartman. I absorbed a lot from him about elements that he valued in pop songs, and they became a part of my own formula. I learned to write for other people but always had a piece of myself, my own point of view, and my own taste in every lyric. That has not changed.

There are different methods of writing songs: lyrics first and then the melody; melody first and then lyrics; or melody and lyrics simultaneously. What is your method? Can you be flexible? By being flexible, I have been able to succeed in many different writing situations. And each method has its own satisfactions. Writing a melody to existing lyrics is the method used by Elton John and Bernie Taupin, and by Dan Hartman and me.

Dan said to me that he loved having a lyric first because it gave him a direction to go in with the music. But he was hard on the lyrics, and in anticipation of him asking for rewrites, I began writing pages of lyrics for him to choose from. I began to love that method, because I discovered that many different variations of a lyric could fit the same song. What was right or wrong? I let my collaborator make that decision—or the director of a movie, or the head of a studio, as happened on the movie set of *Burlesque*.

I was asked to write lyrics for a song in the film *Burlesque* that were to be performed by Cher, a song called "Welcome to Burlesque." I was on the set with the director and the head of the studio knowing that the final decision was going to be made then and there on the lyrics. I came prepared with four pages of words.

The director and the head of the studio got into an argument about which lyric to use, but both agreed that there were many good choices. I also believe that, seeing how much work I had done, they felt that it would be untoward to ask for rewrites. Regardless, they lauded what I had written and continued to argue.

The director then turned to me and asked, "Which lyric do you prefer?" I answered, "I wrote them all; I like them all." The head of the studio won, of course, and, even though I would have been okay with any choice, I think the right choice was made. Thank you, Dan Hartman.

Dan Hartman passed away in 1994 of AIDS-related causes. He was a special, unique talent and friend.

I love writing lyrics first because, as a lyricist, it gives me more latitude to come up with interesting images and words. Melodies without words often limit the sounds and syllables that a lyricist can use. Writing to a melody often makes the lyricist dig even deeper for the right word. It has been said that melody is king, and often that is true. A brilliant melody accompanied by simple words can evoke a response in the manner of great poetry, especially when combined with a transcendent vocal performance.

There is a great song called "You Are So Beautiful," written by Billy Preston and sung by Joe Cocker, that has those three elements and, I believe, reaches those heights. At the end of the song, Joe cannot get out the last note, and it is one of the greatest notes ever sung. It made a great song into a masterpiece. Would those heights have been reached without any one of those elements?

I often write lyrics to existing melodies, because that is the more common procedure. Each method is a different challenge. And today, songwriting has expanded from the model of melodist and lyricist, which still exists, to the model of track person and "topliner." What is a topliner? It is a person who writes the melody and lyrics. I was a topliner for many years and never knew it. My band played the track, and I wrote the melody and lyrics. I was and still am a topliner. Who knew?

The talent for melodies and lyrics does not necessarily exist in the same person. I have spoken to young songwriters who feel pressured to do both when they feel their strengths are solely in one or the other. My advice is always to hone the unique gifts you are given, and try to be nothing less than great. It is a conundrum when you are asked to do a job that you believe does not fit your expertise or your talent. I took a job as a producer, for which I was unprepared and for which I believed was not right for my talent, and it worked out.

Opportunity knocked, and I learned how to do the job in my own way, with my own perspective. Perhaps it was a talent of which I was unaware, or maybe it was my determination to overcome a fear and be up to a challenge, or both.

There are times when there are no easy answers, and you have to make a choice and live with the results. If you are asked to topline and want the gig, then be prepared to write a melody and lyrics or to be clear about your strength and suggest that someone else be brought in to fulfill the need. When I am asked to cowrite, I am always up front about lyrics being my strength and have never been rejected.

Although I can write melodies, I prefer to work with strong melodists like Lauren Christy and Dan Hartman.

Be honest about who you are and what you do. It is both a disarming and welcome approach. If you can deliver the goods as either a melodist or lyricist, the jobs will come. If you feel you can do both, then go forth and deliver the goods. If you want the job as a topliner, regardless of where you feel your talent lies, then go for it, and hopefully you will, as I did, learn on the job. Whatever choice you make, have the courage of your convictions, but be brave and clear eyed enough to recalculate if the decision goes awry.

A person who never made a mistake
never tried anything.

ALBERT EINSTEIN

Songwriting is a gig that most of us learn as we go. There are so many different styles, tastes, and methods of getting to the result of a good song that it is futile to try and create an absolute guideline to being a successful songwriter. However, you can absorb and be influenced by the songs you listen to and people you admire and combine that with your own style, taste, and talent to form your unique voice.

Then, with that unique voice and CRAPP to help you through the emotional roadblocks, you will be in the position to succeed.

EMPATHY

I can't teach you how to write a song, but if you give me your song and I understand the context and your vision, then I believe that I can help that song to reach its potential. That is what I do. I have empathy. Empathy is the ability to understand and share the feelings of another.

It is the ability that, to some degree, every artist who seeks an audience should have. What I am saying is I can sit with you, listen to your song, talk to you, understand where you are coming from, and perhaps help your song somehow. Maybe not—maybe I'm missing something. Maybe you disagree. Fight for what you believe in. But keep an open mind. I personally never disapprove of a collaborator's idea without having a reasonable explanation. "That sucks" is not a reasonable explanation. "That sucks because..." could be a reasonable explanation. But if you have a great, respectful, and trusting relationship with someone, where there are no hidden agendas, then, in order to expedite the situation, you might be in a position to say, "That sucks." I try to reach a mutual comfort level with all my collaborators.

Most of the time, I am successful in doing so because I make it a priority so that I can enjoy the process and it does not feel like work.

I can't teach you how to write a song. There will never be just one method for writing a good song. Every time someone believes that they have figured out *the* formula, a new model appears.

Create something that is personal but universal. A lyric can seem impenetrable but somehow accessible. It touches you. Often there is something in the tenor of a song that affects the listener who barely knows the lyrics. It is a convergence of different elements in the song that creates a deep response with a combination of lyrics, melody, arrangement, and vocals. It is a magic that cannot always be explained.

I know you want to gain knowledge that will help you to succeed, to write a better song, and to give you an edge, as well you should. That is understandable, but you already have something that is more important than any knowledge you will ever gain, and that is your imagination.

There is a well-known, often-quoted phrase attributed to Socrates, sometimes called the Socratic Paradox: "All that I know is that I know nothing." The paradox is that if you know that you know something, then it contradicts that you know nothing. I don't think that he is saying that he does not know anything. He means, instead, that you cannot know anything with absolute certainty but can feel confident about certain things. And I think that's a good philosophical starting point for anyone who is looking for the inner strength to forge ahead when self-doubt creeps into his or her resolve.

My purview is songwriting and record producing, but my point of view on how to attain an emotional edge when chasing your career goal can be useful to anyone who is striving toward a particular career goal. Put all that together with "deserve's got nothing to do with it" and CRAPP, and get inspired.

POSTSCRIPT: KATY, HOLLY, AND KATRINA

The song is called "Watch Me Walk Away," and the artist is named Katrina. My collaborators were Holly Knight and Katy Perry. We wrote it in 2006, when Katy was not yet a world famous superstar. Much to our disappointment, it did not make Katy's album.

Katrina's label heard it and wanted it as a single for Katrina, but Katy's publishing company didn't want to give permission to use it. Katrina's label got angry, and there was somewhat of a minor war. After many heated discussions with various types of threats from Katrina's label, Katy's publisher conceded, but only after Holly had gone through her email and found a letter from Katy giving Holly permission to pitch the song. Chastened, the publisher agreed to issue a "first-use license," but only if Katy's name did not appear as a writer. They did not want anyone riding on Katy's coattails. So Gina Molinari became Katy's nom de plume.

Of course, the moment Katrina's version was released, versions of Katy's demo magically appeared on YouTube—so much for keeping secrets in the era of the internet. Someone in South America even had a copy and put it up on YouTube.

Once again, I had created something, and it resulted in an opportunity, another chance for success. If the song had not been written, if it had not existed, then there would have been no opportunity. As obvious as this reasoning seems to be, I feel that it is a point that needs to be driven home: *put it out there.* And keep on putting it out there to increase your chances for success. Your ideas, your inventions, your songs, your products, your talents—let them live in the world of possibilities. Be productive and proactive. There is no downside. At the least, you will be constantly honing your abilities, learning, and improving your skill—a process that never ends. Yes, I would have preferred to have a hit with Katrina or Katy, or both, but being able to add that story to my repertoire as an instructive anecdote is a good consolation prize.

MONEY CAN'T BUY SUCCESS

My friend and attorney David Rudich asked me to have a meeting with a man and his daughter. She wanted a career as a singer, and he wanted to help her. He was wealthy. She was a teenager. When I met with them, I asked the young lady questions that might have given me some insight into why she wanted this career and how passionate she was about singing. I did not ask her to sing for me. I never got that far.

The girl was barely able to answer a question. Her father gave most of the responses for her. She looked frustrated and uncomfortable. I learned nothing about her motivation. Then her father described the parameters for his daughter's pursuit of a career. She had three months, the length of her summer vacation, to make significant inroads into a singing career. At the end of the three months, if she were not well on her way to a career, then she would be off to college, never to look back.

His daughter looked despondent, and I gave them my usual perspective about the importance of commitment; that although money could buy the best producers, writers, vocal coaches, and mentors, it could not guarantee a successful career; and that a three-month time frame was unrealistic to accomplish anything except starting the process. As if he had not been listening, the father asked if I was interested in getting involved. He never asked if I wanted to hear her sing, and she looked like she wanted to leave. She might have been an amazing talent, but talent is only a small part of the equation for success, and often not the most important. Everyone has some kind of talent. They left, and I never heard her sing; I assume that she went to college.

If I could have heard her answers to my questions as well as her voice, I might have been able to feel strong enough about her potential to offer some help. I love working with young talent and was rooting for her to interrupt her father and assert her passion for singing and her dream of a career in music. Having a successful career of any kind takes a commitment that ignores the odds and is propelled by passion and ambition and is most often achieved with persistence. It could possibly happen in three months, or even less, if the angel of insane luck smiles on you, or if your father buys the company—a suggestion I did not think of at the time. But I still would have first wanted to hear her sing. Money can't buy everything.

Even if you've got the funds to help you in your career, there is no guarantee of success. Setting a time frame is not a bad thing if you have a sense of humor about it. One time frame leads to another and another and another. Then when you give up setting time limits for reaching your success, it happens. You have persisted until you succeeded. Setting goals is constructive. Setting time limits is destructive.

Chapter Ten
GIVING AND TAKING CRITICISM

Choosing to deliver criticism is like deciding to cross a frozen lake with no assurance that you won't crash through the ice and drown. First, you have to be sure that it is necessary to criticize. Then you have to make a judgment as to the best route. If you have taken this journey before, then you probably have a good idea of the path you should take. However, there are no guarantees that you will make a successful crossing: there is always a risk.

You have to establish that your criticism is not meant to disparage but, instead, to open up the possibility that there might be a better choice. Make sure that you are criticizing the idea and not the person, and then begin and end your critique with positive words about the person's idea and the person.

Your criticism should not seem like a criticism. It should appear to be, and actually is, suggesting another alternative. That is my approach, and it is grounded in the humility I have developed after years of working with so many talented people with so many good ideas.

Conversely, learning to accept criticism will be important for nurturing strong collaborations and relationships. I acknowledge that being the object of criticism is always personal. I used to bristle when someone who was about to criticize my work or me said, "Please don't take this personally." That is the perfectly wrong approach to having someone accept or even listen your criticism. And a critique can also be positive. Treat both the negatives and the positives with equal skepticism. Concentrate on whether you feel the opinion resonates with you. If you are satisfied with your creation or your idea, then it will be because you have been your own critic, continually assessing it until, by your own rigid standards, you are satisfied with the result.

Taking in criticism with an open mind can be beneficial to your work. If you adopt that attitude, then you will welcome the comments as possibly being able to provide a fresh and useful perspective.

There is no way you can be harmed by criticism if you believe in what you have done and remember that you are the final arbiter, able to accept or reject any criticism. Understand that only the work, and not you, is being critiqued. Negative or positive, a critique of your work does not decrease or increase your value as a person. It is always personal, because you have invested your time, creativity, taste, talent, and emotion in your work. Take pride in what you have created and all the personal elements it took to get to that result, but never let your pride get in the way of your determination to get the best results.

Objective criticism does not exist. Every professional and nonprofessional critic has formed criteria for his or her criticism based on taste, education, experience, influences, and the mood of the times in which he or she lives. We are born with certain dispositions that also might influence how we react to the world around us and how our senses and sensibilities are affected. There are no absolute truths when it comes to defining the worthiness of a piece of work: it is always subjective. But there is value in listening closely to an opinion that you can accept or reject in whole or in part. Even if you reject that opinion, you might gain an insight that could help your creativity to grow. Maintain your cool, be a good listener, keep an open mind, and focus on what you think is best for your work.

I produced an album for Joe Cocker called *One Night of Sin*. The title of the album was taken from the original title of a Dave Bartholomew song that was a hit for Elvis Presley that was retitled "One Night with You." The album was a success, and the song "When the Night Comes" (Bryan Adams, Diane Eve Warren, James Douglas Vallance) won a Grammy nomination for Joe for best rock vocal performance and was his last hit. The album went platinum and gold in many countries around the world.

In *Rolling Stone* magazine, Jim Farber wrote this about the album:

> [One Night of Sin] *was too slick and conformist for Cocker, but at least producers Charlie Midnight and Dan Hartman stripped away a few of the fattier elements, giving the old growl some leeway. Now Midnight has managed to undo everything good that was accomplished last time.*

James Chrispell from *AllMusic* had this to say about the album:

> With One Night of Sin, *Joe Cocker and his cohorts decided not to mess with the hit formula they had found with* Unchain My Heart. *Therefore,* One Night of Sin *suffers a bit in comparison. However, that's not to say that this isn't great '80s Joe Cocker, because everything here has something to recommend it.*

CD Universe said this:

> One Night of Sin, *Cocker apparently relates to the sexual paranoia in Leonard Cohen's "I'm Your Man," and he gives it an appropriately volcanic rendering. Even better, he seems to locate a similar feeling of dread in the old Little Willie John/Peggy Lee chestnut "Fever," and he positively out-Elvis's Elvis with his take on the similarly themed title song. Guilt never sounded so good.*

The *Rolling Stone* review was like getting hit in the head with a baseball bat, except that you might recover from the baseball bat, and for a moment, I was not sure if I would recover from the review. In fact, I had been unintentionally bashed with a baseball bat during a game of softball in the schoolyard at Seth Low Junior High School in Bensonhurst. I was playing the catcher's position, and the batter stepped too far back in the batter's box. He took a swing at a pitch, and before his bat could meet the pitch, it made contact with my head. I have no recollection of the moments between getting hit and awakening, surrounded by my friends, some looking concerned and some laughing. A large swelling grew on my head, and somebody said, "Let's get him to a doctor." The real pain did not come until later that night. There was no blood, and the swelling had not yet fully blossomed. My team was ahead, and it was the penultimate inning. I got up, found my baseball cap—which had flown a few feet away—crouched behind the plate, and said, "Screw that. Play ball."

That has become my attitude when hit with skull-bashing criticism. "Screw that. Play ball."

Treat published reviews, if you are courageous enough to read them, the same way you treat criticism from collaborators, friends, passersby, relatives, or whoever offers an opinion that enters your consciousness. Understand that it is subjective but that there might be a useful kernel of insight to be digested. And there might not be. The positive aspect of being critiqued by a stranger in a publication is that you do not have to respond to the criticism. You do not have to be sensitive and concerned with the state of the collaboration or relationship. If the review is good, then you can cut it out of the publication or print it out from your computer, frame it, and hang it on your wall. If the review is negative, you can burn the publication or banish it from your computer. Or you can treat them equally and hang both on the wall as souvenirs from your journey.

Each of those three reviews has a different, subjective take on the album. Again, there is no objective criterion that informs all critiques. The album survived the *Rolling Stone* review and went on to commercial success and a Grammy nomination for Joe Cocker. But I had already rebounded from the *Rolling Stone* review before the album's success. I had kept my passion burning and persisted through all the obstacles and disappointments and had just produced my second Joe Cocker album. A bad review could not keep me from being proud of how far I had come and the work I had done—from believing in myself.

Chapter Eleven
HINDSIGHT IS 20/20

These are some thoughts that I formed after I had achieved success. Only then was I able to have the clarity of vision that is achieved with hindsight.

- Stay engaged in life, and you'll stay young forever. Disengage, and you become old.
- If you believe that your destiny is written in the stars or in some celestial book and is somehow preordained, then that would assume that successful people are the "chosen ones." It becomes easy, then, for the "failures" to accept their lots because it simply "wasn't meant to be." This might ease the pain of not achieving your goal, but it is not conducive to having the determination to persist.
- I was living on Brighton First Place, one block from the L and the D train, thinking that maybe I was one of those people who never "makes it" in the way that "making it" is often defined in the music business: becoming a star. I

had spent over a decade in the trenches and was wondering whether I should continue. Finding the resolve and strength to continue in the face of that frustration, doubt, and poverty was the cauldron out of which my survival philosophy was formed.

- Don't have a backup plan. Throw yourself into the deep end, and learn how to swim.

- It is important for your emotional survival to learn how to live your life while you are pursuing your dream. Then, when your pursuit has ended and you are at the place where you dreamed you would be, it will be a revelation that, all the while, you *have* been living your dream.

- Charisma in a voice has always been more important to a successful singing career than "chops."

- When the door opens, do not hesitate; go through it, act as if you know what you are doing, and count on your intelligence and wits to carry you through. If you fake it long enough, then, eventually, you *will* know what you are doing.

- If you are fortunate enough to understand what your gift is, then do not take it for granted. Work on it. Hone it. It is a muscle that you need to exercise and build to its potential.

- If your road to success was smooth, be prepared: there will be rough times ahead. One way or the other, you are going to pay your dues. First, you need to dream before you can succeed.

- Originality, if it exists, is overrated. In any field, there is always a place for another great song, product, or idea. Excellence is far more important than originality.

- The honest passion for what you do, for your work, is a magnet that will attract others to you.
- If your passion and creativity never grow old, then you will stay forever young.
- Never impugn your integrity as a person or as an artist.
- Keep an open mind, and give someone else's ideas a chance. Making compromises in a collaboration does not mean that you are compromising your ideals or integrity.
- Put your truth and uniqueness out there, and your true and unique success will find you.
- Don't say what you think people want to hear. Say what you believe, but choose your words with care and tact.
- People respond to passion. Express yourself passionately with intelligence, and people will listen.
- Do what you do best, if you can figure that out.
- People often go after careers that they think they should pursue, rather than careers based on their talents and what work gives them satisfaction.
- Looking at other people's success and trying to figure out "why them and not me" is a thankless exercise that can make you rotten with cynicism and result in defeatism— two isms that will block your road to success.
- Forget about it being easy. Set your sights, enjoy the process, and get your satisfaction in the doing; when done with one project, move on to the next.
- Do not feel that you are in competition with anyone. You are unique. There is always room for one more unique talent, regardless of how crowded the field may be.

The world owes you nothing but the life you were given,

so go out, work toward what you want, and keep your fingers crossed that a building doesn't fall on you as you make your way.

Open up that channel to your creativity. Free yourself. Let that inspiration flow that is not encumbered by wondering what the outcome should be. Get it started. What creates writer's block is being too concerned, and being stuck on "what this should or shouldn't be." Inspiration must come first. Your inspiration of the moment, the spark that ignites your creative fire, will let you survive until the next moment, and the next, until, once again, your creative fire is raging.

What part should luck play in the formula for success? None. Sometimes it can be a factor in success, but it is too arbitrary and out of your control to be included in any formula.

However, it can befall anyone, so why not you? Leave it out of your formula, because expecting to get lucky can weaken your resolve to follow the plan and can make you lazy. I would rather you believe that you achieved your success through your own collaborations, relationships, ambition, persistence, and passion than to believe you simply got lucky. Furthermore, I do not believe that "you make your own luck." Luck is not created by your efforts, but by chance. And chance is an unreliable ally.

Epilogue

THE DEED,
TEN YEARS LÁTER

In 2010, I was asked to produce a band in Zurich, Switzerland, fronted by the Swiss artist known as Gölä. The band was called The Deed, and consisted of the musicians who had, for years, been playing shows and recording with Gölä. This album would be their debut as a group, and the album would be a rock album comprised of classic-style rock songs all sung by Gölä in English. He had huge success writing and singing songs in Swiss German, but a previous album in English he'd released on his own was less successful. Stylistically, the album I was called on to co-write and produce would also be a departure for Gölä. Still, it was his dream to record and write this kind of classic rock album, and so, there I was in the mountains of Zurich in a large recording studio with a band of nonpareil musicians ready to rock.

The studio was in a large complex that housed Balik Farm, a producer of prime smoked salmon, located in the alps of the

Toggenburg region in Switzerland, in the town of Ebersol. It was an idyllic, pastoral setting, and the building had rooms for the band to stay while recording. We were feasted every night by our German chef, Laetitia Moser, who, after I made it known that I do not like the taste of alcohol save for the impossibly sweet German Ice Wine, brought a bottle of that wine to the next night's dinner.

One of the owners was a musician and built his dream studio —a dream studio with a dream band, a dream chef, and a dream environment. It was the perfect prelude to the release of an album by the most successful recording artist in Switzerland. There seemed to be a consensus by those involved with the project—including the record company, the manager, the band, and anyone who had heard the recordings—that this was going to be a hit album. Representatives of the label had traveled to the studio to feast with us and departed singing the music's praises. All the right factors seemed to be in place. And then the album never came out.

There were politics involved, Gölä prioritized other projects, and for a few years I held out hope. It was a deep disappointment, but I had learned to not let these kinds of disappointments lessen the satisfaction of the experience. The hurt dissipates and disappears. I did not let the unanticipated, hollow ending to the project obliterate the fullness of the joy I felt from the music we made, and the camaraderie and the sense of purpose I shared with the band Gölä, Walter Keiser (Drums), Martin Chabloz (Keyboards), Ueli Bleuler (Guitar), Peter Keiser (Bass), and John Woolloff (Guitar). And Alexandre Bolle, the engineer; Lukas Moser, the manager; and Laetitia Moser, the chef and my personal sommelier. The intense, fruitful creativity, the beauty of the alpine landscape, the scrumptious culinary nights—each of these experiences were ends in themselves and those are the positive feelings that have stayed with me.

Now and then through the years I would listen to the album and the good memories and the recordings would give me great pleasure and buoy my spirits despite a sigh or two that it had not seen the light of day. The failure of the album to come out was not a failure of the album itself, but a matter of circumstances that I could not control. What I could control was to view it as a successful sojourn in my circuitous emotional and creative journey.

Then, ten years after my dreamlike stopover at Balik Farm, where recording music meshes with world-renowned smoked salmon, I received a message from Gölä that the album, entitled *Hour of the Thief* was being released in Switzerland in June, 2020, accompanied by substantial promotion and a long-form video entailing Gölä's journey through Australia in 2011 to promote the album that was then not released.

Of course, I hope the album finds a big audience, but I have for many years now been satisfied with the profound emotional and creative fulfillment I felt, and still feel, from that recording and my days in Switzerland. I moved on years ago from the expectations of any release happening, let alone expecting the album to be a hit. But, as Bella would say, "It couldn't hurt."

I hope you take something similar from this book, that you're able to strip away all the rationalizations and defenses built up by all the disappointments, and go back to the beginning: return to the reason why. Get the creative juices flowing, and enter that transcendent state of mind that raises your consciousness, heightens your senses, takes you out of whatever darkness you might have been in, and leads you to a place of light. It is a gift we are given to be able to love what we work at—what our talent allows us to do—so that, when we immerse ourselves in it, we are lifted to a higher place, which might even be described as bliss. For a while, we forget that sometimes the process did not feel so good, that the struggle to create something satisfying was often too frustrating and left us with the feeling of being less than. The struggle is important, because each time you get through it and are not defeated, it strengthens your belief in your own worth.

And one more thing—I know I wrote that this is not a motivational book, and that is true, but if something in these pages has motivated you to follow your heart into a career about which you are passionate, then I would also say not to let anyone give you crap and tell you that you cannot do it. Whatever path you choose, I am giving you CRAPP, with two Ps, and telling you that you can and will do it.

CRAPP—collaboration, relationships, ambition, passion, and persistence—five elements that, when combined with your talent, will help you achieve your success. And even though deserve's got nothing to do with it, your success will be well deserved.

And then on Wednesday, June 17, 2020, The Deed's album, *Hour of the Thief,* entered the Swiss charts at Number Three.

AFTERWORD

When I started writing this book, there was no global epidemic threatening the existences and earning power of millions of people. But, as I was putting the finishing touches on my book, the COVID-19 virus had changed the landscape for every touring and studio musician, recording studio, engineer, studio singer--anyone and any entity that depended on being able to be in their place of work and to be in that space with other workers and clients. So many of these talented people who devoted their lives and businesses to their passions had been waylaid. The gig economy as a whole had been put in dire straits. I am optimistic that when this book comes out, the worst will be behind us. The vaccines that have been developed and those that are soon to come should bring the relief that we desperately need. As I write this, at the beginning of the year 2021, I am comforted by these hopefully prescient lines from Alfred, Lord Tennyson: "Hope smiles from the threshold of the year to come, whispering 'It will be happier.'"

Buck Johnson, a multitalented artist, songwriter, pianist, and producer from Shady Grove, Alabama, who I met years ago when he moved to L.A. with his wife, Kym, a former Miss Alabama, was one of the people whose life had been adversely affected. In 2005, Buck had some success, including cowriting, with Jamie Houston and Damon Johnson, the hit song, "Just Feel Better," with vocals by Steven Tyler, from the Santana album, *All That I Am.* In 2007, he was part of the country band called Whiskey Falls, and they released an album on Midas Records that made it to number 25 on the country charts. They disbanded after a few years.

Throughout the time that Buck was in LA, we wrote and recorded many songs together with the intent of one day releasing a Buck Johnson album, which we did in 2016 on his self-titled album that I coproduced with the legendary mixer and producer Mark Needham. The album didn't get much traction and soon, Buck and Kym moved to Nashville, where he auditioned and got the gig as keyboardist and backing vocalist for Aerosmith. Then he was enlisted for The Hollywood Vampires. For years, the shows kept him busy and earning a good living as well as increasing his profile for the next album, which he was already working on with the magic of digital recording in his hotel rooms.

Then it stopped. And this was the same scenario in different ways for so many others.

Surviving financially and emotionally until we got to the "new normal" that allowed everyone to get back to work in whatever form this new normal would take was the objective. Buck kept his creativity flowing by going into a studio and recording his new album, then filming videos of stripped down versions of the songs with the musicians in different locations. He also posted videos of himself doing unplugged versions of some of the many songs he had written through the years, and we have continued to write together.

Keeping your passion and drive undiminished while figuring out how to earn a living is its own job. It is a continuing, fluid process to which we are committed. I was in the studio producing a few sessions during the surge and it gave me great satisfaction to be able to hire musicians. The safety protocols in the studio were strictly adhered to. Buck was in the process of signing with a publisher who heard his unreleased album and got excited about working with him. He was doing what was needed for his emotional survival as well as using every possible avenue to increase the possibility of earning income from his talent. The optimal outcome would be that when this book is released, the pandemic will have abated, with Buck returned to concert venues with Aerosmith and the Hollywood Vampires and that the efforts he made under great pressure to earn income from his music have paid off and continue to do so. Pressure can be a positive force when it drives you to find new ways to survive, and new avenues that you would never have explored were it not for the pressure and new directions that take you out of your comfort zone—especially if you continue to use them as you move forward

In the middle of the COVID-19 pandemic, surviving your emotional journey to whatever success meant to you became even more urgent. That meaning might have been altered to some degree by this unique hardship, but the elements needed to get there—collaboration, relationships, ambition, passion, and persistence--remained constant. And, in the midst of this adversity, when you added some ingenuity and out-of-the-box thinking to CRAPP, you were left unbowed by COVID-19.

ABOUT THE AUTHOR

Charlie Midnight was born in Brooklyn, and raised in Bensonhurst. After years of gigging in bars and clubs and an unsuccessful album on Columbia Records, Charlie survived to become a successful record producer/songwriter for such artists as James Brown's Grammy-nominated "Living in America," Joe Cocker's "Trust in Me," and *The Bodyguard,* the bestselling soundtrack album of all time. Charlie also worked with Joni Mitchell on "How Do You Stop" for her Grammy-winning album, *Turbulent Indigo;* as well as Jamey Johnson, "My Way to You," for his Grammy-winning album, *The Guitar Song*. He collaborated with Barbra Streisand on "I Still Can See Your Face," a duet with Andrea Bocelli, for her Grammy-winning album, *Duets.*

Deserve's Got Nothing To Do With It is Charlie's first book. His short story, "The Tire Iron," will appear in the 2020 winter edition of *Calliope Literary Magazine,* the official publication of the Writers' Special Interest Group (SIG) of American Mensa, Ltd. Charlie is currently working on a novel, *The Gig*, a love triangle between the lead singer for the worst bar band in Brooklyn, a soft-core porn actress, and a low-level, local "Good Guy."

ACKNOWLEDGMENTS

There are people and situations that inspired me to write this book and helped me to stay the course on my journey to completion. My editors at Mascot: Kristin Perry, who spent many hours with me on the phone going over what I had written and respecting my voice in the writing, giving sage suggestions to cohere my style and content. Emily Temple, who stepped in as production editor to finish the editing, the physical configuration, and overall look of the book. Lauren Magnussen, who in the last phase took over for Emily. I want to thank Naren Aryal, the founder of Mascot and friend of writers for his availability to me, encouragement, and reassurance. Anne McNamara, my first editor, who when I originally had the idea for the book offered me encouragement and early guidance. Jeff Rabhan, Chair of the Clive Davis Institute, for thinking my idea for the book and especially my title, *Deserve's Got Nothing To Do With It: Talking CRAPP With Charlie Midnight*, was a winner, regardless of whether he meant it or not. Peter Hirsch, noted author of many bestselling books including *Living the Significant Life*, for his enthusiasm about my book in its early draft and advising me on how to best move forward with it. Mark Bryan bestselling author of many books, including *The Artist's Way at Work*, for believing that I had something worthwhile to say with this book.

Royce Gorsuch, who took the time to read the book as it was evolving and whose positive reaction to its message energized me to keep moving forward.

Jenny Roa, who told me how inspired she was by the book which gave me even more confidence—not only that it could resonate with readers but that it was an enjoyable read.

The students who attended my lectures at The Clive Davis Institute and The Syracuse University Los Angeles Extension, for their warm and excited response to what I had to say, much of which helped me solidify the philosophies and perspectives that are the foundation of why I wrote *Deserve's Got Nothing To Do With It.*